# EUROPE'S FUTURES,
# EUROPE'S CHOICES

W9-CHC-197

# EUROPE'S FUTURES, EUROPE'S CHOICES

*Models of Western Europe in the 1970s*

Edited by

ALASTAIR BUCHAN

COLUMBIA UNIVERSITY PRESS

NEW YORK

*for*

THE INSTITUTE FOR STRATEGIC STUDIES

LONDON

Columbia University Press Edition

*First printing 1969*
*Second printing 1971*

ISBN 0–231–08627-X
Library of Congress Catalog Card Number: 77-83385
Printed in the United States of America

# CONTENTS

# PREFACE

This is a moment of slack water in the tide of European affairs, of uncertainty and of frustration. The clarity that the Cold War imposed upon relations between the countries of the developed world, in particular the sense of solidarity within each of the two main alliances, has become blurred; the assumption of a natural community of interest between the nations of the Atlantic world has been weakened, and so has an equivalent sense of identity between Eastern Europe and the Soviet Union; the belief that economic association within Western Europe would lead naturally to political association has been called in question; and many traditional sources of division between the European powers, nationalism and diminishing confidence in governments, which were muted through much of the postwar era, have begun to reassert themselves.

This uncertainty which shrouds the future of European relations presents a difficult problem of methodology for a research centre concerned with, among other subjects, questions of security and stability in Europe. For any analysis of the future structure of relations between the European powers, and the motive forces that will predominate, let alone Europe's relations with the wider world, that relies solely on an extrapolation of the trends of the late 1960s into the 1970s is, if given any precision, likely to lead to miscalculation and false prophecy or, if cautious, to emerge merely as a series of wide generalizations which have little value as a guide to policy and choice.

ISS, like other institutes, has found it more illuminating to take a step into the future and examine a number of different forms of association between the West European powers that could develop in the next decade. The purpose of this study is threefold: first, to examine different structures of a future Western Europe, in order to see what their effects would be, especially on the Atlantic Alliance and on East–West relations; second, to assess the possibilities each of them offers for the solution of Europe's own problems: third, to bring out the choices which will confront policy-makers in the coming years. For, as Professor Daniel Bell has said:

> Planning, by its very nature, is not a mechanical process. Central to it is the problem of choice – both for the ends desired and for the allocation of resources. Thus planning and rationality are one. All this puts us on the threshold of an ancient and persistent human quest: to choose our futures. And what is central, therefore, to the present future studies is not an effort to 'predict' the future, as if this were some far-flung rug of time unrolled to some distant point, but the effort to sketch 'alternative futures' – in other words, the likely results of different choices, so that the polity can understand the costs and consequences of different desires.[1]

This study has many shortcomings but it has been subjected to a rigorous process of international criticism in the course of writing. We owe a considerable debt of gratitude to a diverse group of European and American scholars and officials, not least to our colleagues Kenneth Hunt and Curt Gasteyger, who have extended our vision by discussing and commenting on our ideas at various stages in the construction of these models and the analysis of their implications. In particular I would like to pay tribute to the work of three of our Research Associates, Christoph Bertram, Peter Ramsbotham, and Walther Stützle, who, together with myself, have borne the primary responsibility for the development of this study.

November 1968                                    Alastair Buchan

---

[1] Herman Kahn and Anthony J. Wiener, *The Year 2,000* (New York: Macmillan; London: Collier-Macmillan, for the Hudson Institute, 1967), Introduction by Professor Daniel Bell, p. xxvi.

Introduction

# THE FRAMEWORK OF
# EUROPEAN CHOICE

I

The only fact about the future that anyone can predict with
assurance is the advance of time. The most certain development
of the 1970s is the change in the historical environment of those
who will be politically influential – in Western Europe or elsewhere. By the beginning of the 1970s the political significance
of those, whether leaders or voters, who remember the First
World War will be waning rapidly, and by the end of the
decade it will have disappeared. At the other end of the scale,
those who have no memory of the political and economic
conditions of the 1930s and only a child's fragmented recollec-
tion of the origins of the Cold War that is, (those born after
1940) will, by 1970, comprise nearly a quarter of the voters in
West European countries. By 1980 theirs will be the dominant
age group, and it will be providing many of the leaders in
politics and industry. Moreover, the 1970s will not be very far
advanced when a generation whose memory of even the later
days of the Cold War, the Cuban missile crisis or the last Berlin crisis, is hazy or derivative, becomes eligible to vote and
acquires political significance.

These new political generations will, of course, fragment
according to interests and convictions, very possibly along the
same lines of class, regional or economic motive as the preceding ones. Moreover, men's fears or interests are derived not
only from what they can recall directly, but also from what
they are taught. But, assuming that Europe does not revert to
open conflict, the growing influence of men and women who
did not live through the thirty years of 'Europe's civil war'
from 1914 to 1945, or who remember 'the Cold War only as

history', is likely to give rise to an increased questioning in most West European countries of the conventional wisdom of the previous generation, embodied in such phrases as 'Atlantic community', 'the iron curtain', 'the containment of Germany'. This does not mean that the political realities that lie behind these phrases may not endure. What it does mean is that European governments will no longer be able to take popular acceptance of such concepts for granted.

A second political factor has made itself felt in West European politics in the later 1960s, and seems likely to persist into the 1970s, namely a growing alienation of popular support from governments and a rising dissatisfaction with existing political institutions. As the problem of governing a capitalist-welfare state becomes increasingly complex, as bureaucracies have to intervene in more and more sectors of national life, as central government appears increasingly remote and hard to influence, so there is developing a debate about national political institutions, epitomized in the catchword 'participation'. Scepticism about the established political order shows signs of extending to international institutions, at least to the extent of diminishing faith in their value.

Thus, to the familiar difficulty of guessing who may be the leaders of Western Europe in the next decade – for a conjunction of Roy Jenkins, Helmut Schmidt and Edgar Faure might produce very different solutions from one of Edward Heath, Franz Joseph Strauss and Georges Pompidou – a new uncertainty about the political temper and direction of West European societies has been added. The student unrest which affected virtually all of Western Europe, and the United States and much of Eastern Europe as well, in 1967 and 1968, may or may not be transitory; but it has reminded the generation that now wields power, the generation that lived through the Cold War, that its own values and priorities, its belief in national security and prosperity and regional co-operation as prime objectives, are not absolute and may be challenged. 'Nothing begets change' it was said with reference to the 1870s 'like a change of generation.'

2

There is a related factor which may accentuate the current trend of national introspection, in Europe as elsewhere. If the unrest among students and organized labour that was evident in the late 1960s should persist – and it may not – it will create a series of social tensions and present problems of public order that can be alleviated only by national authorities. The international affiliations of governments will be irrelevant to these groups, if they are not a positive drawback and target for attack. The assumption of the Monnetistes that a single culture is developing among the younger generation in Western Europe may also come to appear questionable.

On the other hand, the similarity of the social and political problems in different European countries, indeed in the advanced industrial states as a whole, could produce a new kind of internationalism, as the West European states move, at varying speeds, towards what has been called a post-industrial society. Concern with the structure, range and content of higher education; the search for new techniques of democratic participation in political decision-making; the problems of the cities, of urban renewal; the problems, in some countries at least, of a multi-racial community; the problem of reconciling human needs with the impact of a technological society. These are all basically similar and experience in one country affects the decisions of another.

Moreover, the tendency to concentrate on purely national solutions to the political and social problems in Western Europe may be contradicted by the necessities of economic and technological progress. For one thing, all the West European countries are developing mass consumption economies which set limits on the amount of resources governments can divert from the private to the public sector, except for purposes that provide a direct return to the individual, such as welfare. The need for the most economical use of public resources could lead to new forms of international co-operation or division of labour in such fields as defence, energy and the high-technology industries.

To this general need is added Western Europe's particular

3

problem of confronting the technological power of the United States and, during the 1970s, of Japan. Much has been written about *Le Défi américain* – the title of Jean-Jacques Servan-Schreiber's influential book – some of it confusing the problem of rising American investment in and control of advanced industry in Europe, and the competitive power of American domestic products in world markets. Whether the problem of American investment in Europe will remain as acute in the 1970s as in the later 1960s is not clear and present indications suggest that it may not.[1] But nothing is likely to diminish the competitive power of the American science-based industries, which rests not only on a high quality of management and larger companies than in Europe, but also on a base of trained scientific manpower three times as large as that of the whole of Western Europe, including Sweden. To maintain a position of reasonable economic strength, sufficient to prevent a gradual poisoning of European–American relations, may necessitate not only the minimizing of internal trade barriers in Europe, already begun by EEC and EFTA within their own systems, but novel techniques of international co-operation between both industries and governments, although this may be bilateral rather than comprehensive in the first instance.

But it is the monetary factor that creates the strongest element of interdependence, not only within Western Europe but in the Atlantic community as a whole, and which limits many choices theoretically open to European governments. In theory, they could consciously choose a declining share of world trade and a declining rate of domestic economic growth in order to preserve their national autonomy, or avoid the disagreeable choices involved in becoming a technological society. But the financial crises of the late 1960s have shown how closely the value of Western currencies is intertwined. That the international monetary system of the non-Communist advanced states will need reform in the next decade is now a common-

[1] See 'Plant and Equipment Expenditures by Foreign Affiliates of U.S. Firms' – Revised Estimates 1967 and 1968, *Survey of Current Business*, May 1968, p. 14.

place among governments, but what form it will take is uncertain and is a further justification for discussing the future structure of Western Europe in terms of alternative choices rather than attempting to predict it.

But the general social, political and economic trends of the late 1960s point merely to the likelihood of change in the values and priorities of Western governments in the 1970s. They give no clear indication of the direction of that change; whether, for instance, social and political scepticism will assume a national or a trans-national form; whether economic and social values will be seen to conflict, and if so which will predominate; whether the new modes of co-operation, that economic and other pressures may force governments to adopt, will be based on an intrinsic sense of Europeanism or merely on a sense of common external threat; or whether such co-operation will emerge at all.

II

If the trends within Western Europe provide no clear guidance about the way in which its political and economic association may develop, whether Europe will stand still or unite, the developments in the structure of international relations as a whole provide no certain answer either. Anyone who attempts to examine the external forces which will affect the West European countries in the 1970s, and the structural changes in their relations which may result, is immediately confronted with a range of uncertainties which can be summarized under four headings.

(1) The first concerns the relationship of the two superpowers. Clearly their interest in avoiding direct conflict with each other is likely to persist. But in 1968 it is impossible to be sure whether impending developments in the technology of strategic deterrence, when coupled with difficulties of creating a stable balance of interests in Asia and the Middle East, will lead to a deterioration in relations between Washington and

Moscow, or will force them towards some form of *modus vivendi* based on mutual restraint.

(2) Related to this is the uncertainty as to how much authority the two super-powers will wish and be able to maintain within their respective European alliance systems. This involves two elements. How much will their leadership be respected – there has, after all, been a marked diminution in the respect paid in Europe to the views of both Washington and Moscow? And to what extent will they continue to feel that strategic considerations (and ideological considerations in the case of the Soviet Union) require a pre-eminent position for themselves in their respective alliances and a centralized system of command and control? The events of August 1968 in Czechoslovakia certainly suggest that at least the Soviet Union still does. But, in the long run, the answer is intimately bound up with the first question; a continuation of *détente* in super-power relations in Europe will not necessarily enhance their authority there, while the converse, hardened relations, might lead to a kind of neutralism, at least in Western Europe.

(3) Then there is the uncertainty as to where developments within Eastern Europe are leading. While the Soviet Union has made it plain that she will continue to fear and to resist change within her bloc, the extent to which her satellites will abide by her command is unclear; it may at least vary from country to country – some resisting change, others seeking internal liberalization, others even risking open dissent.

(4) Most important of all for our purposes is the range of uncertainties that surrounds the future of Western Europe and the attitude of its component states to the East, to the United States and to each other. Though it is a reasonable assumption that President de Gaulle will have left office before the 1970s are very old, we have little firm evidence as to whether he will leave a permanent imprint on French policy. The present Eastern policy of the German Government, the appearance of a growing consensus on developing some new relationship with East Germany, even if it involves *de facto* recognition in the 1970s, a diminishing interest in strengthening the Western

6

organizations of which Germany is a part, may not survive a change in the balance of political forces within Germany herself. Britain has taken a series of decisions which emphasize her relationship with Europe, but if this leads to no strengthening of institutional relationships with her neighbours, other alternatives, perhaps the construction of an Anglo-Saxon bloc in world politics and trade, may begin to attract support.

## III

But to gain any clear picture of the choices open to Western Europe in the next decades, one must proceed from certain assumptions about the environment of international politics, most particularly about the relations between the two super-powers. By 1967 one fact had become apparent, namely that developments in the technology of strategic offence and defence could undermine the stability that the creation of large, relatively secure, retaliatory systems in each country has provided. The development of ballistic missile defence systems to the point where it is worth discussing their operational deployment, multiple warheads for ICBMs to facilitate penetration of such a defence system or orbital weapons to evade them, advances in submarine detection, and uncertainty as to the level of strategic forces at which each power is aiming, mean that Soviet–American relations in the first half of the 1970s could be dominated by the same kinds of uncertainty as in the late 1950s and early 1960s. If this were so, it could not fail to affect Europe, probably producing in some countries an enhanced sense of solidarity with their respective super-power and in others neutralism, but almost certainly postponing the prospects of any general modification of the Continent's twenty-year military confrontation.

But there are also signs, still tentative, that both countries are anxious to avoid the costs as well as the risks of exploiting all the possibilities that military technology has provided or of taking a major step forward in their strategic arms race. It was, for instance, clear by 1967 that many of those responsible for the higher direction of American defence policy would like to find a formula that permitted the stabilization of the super-power balance and were prepared to consider foregoing American numerical superiority in strategic weapons in the interests of long-term stability. In June 1968 Mr Gromyko announced the Soviet Government's readiness to explore the question further, almost certainly reflecting Soviet concern at the economic costs of an indefinite competition in strategic weapons.

Of course willingness to negotiate does not ensure a successful outcome, and there are powerful political interests in both countries opposed to any agreement whether formal or informal, tacit or explicit. But it is clear that the super-powers now face the prospect of either finding some common ground on the strategic aspect of the central balance of power which they maintain, or else, in all probability, losing influence within their alliance systems and power to control crises in Europe and elsewhere, which might bring them into direct conflict with each other. So that even if there is some deterioration in Soviet–American relations in the early 1970s, as a consequence of strategic developments, the decade may not progress very far without their reaching some understanding in this sphere.

But a common effort to preserve *détente* may not necessarily result in *entente*, for the United States and the Soviet Union are still the centres of two basically antithetical economic and political systems. Moreover, even if there is some convergence in their attitudes to arms control, and even if they find some common ground in the area of European security, their interests conflict in the Middle East, and may conflict sharply elsewhere if the Soviet Union pursues, as the diversification of her military forces suggests she may, a more ambitious role in Asia and elsewhere, outside her traditional sphere of interests.

Certainly it seems improbable that China will achieve sufficient external or strategic power during the 1970s to force the two existing super-powers into a working partnership, or that she could sufficiently threaten the security of either to the point

8

where they must close ranks and settle their differences in Europe. In recent years there has been a continuous over-estimation of China's capabilities, both at home and abroad, a tendency 'to multiply', as Herman Kahn has put it, 'anything that happens in China by eight hundred million, as if the six hundred million or so Chinese peasants (as opposed to the two hundred million or so urbanized Chinese) constitute an overwhelming physical, economic, moral or political force in world affairs'.[2]

China will have a strategic nuclear force of some kind during the 1970s: she will exert an increasing influence on Asian politics, and, assuming that there is no rapprochement between Peking and Moscow, there may gradually evolve a division of labour between Moscow and Washington in containing and deterring her: the one assuming the preponderant role in the Indian sub-continent and the other in the Pacific. But China possesses no magic power to transform Soviet–American relations in Europe over the next few years.

The first assumption of this study is that Western Europe will have to make a series of choices about its internal organization and its relation with the super-powers in a period in which their hostility may be muted and controlled, but in which no clear alternative to a Soviet–American balance of power is visible. The implications of this assumption will be explored in the chapters on the different models. In July 1968 the Non-Proliferation Treaty was signed by the United States, the Soviet Union and Britain, while France's representative at the United Nations had earlier said that 'France will conduct herself in this field exactly like the states who decide to sign.' All the European non-nuclear powers, East and West, may eventually sign, although the Soviet occupation of Czechoslovakia in August 1968 will not have encouraged them. This has a double corollary for Europe: first, it rules out certain conceptions of a European nuclear force, since the treaty forbids

[2] Herman Kahn and Anthony J. Wiener, *The Year 2,000* (New York: MacMillan; London: Collier-MacMillan, for the Hudson Institute, 1967), p. 230.

the transference of warheads or of information about their construction from nuclear to non-nuclear powers; second, it should remove from the agenda of international debate the possibility that Germany or Italy might become nuclear powers during the 1970s; though, since the NPT might break down if it fails to control the danger of proliferation worldwide, it does not rule out such a possibility in the more distant future. On the other hand, there is nothing in the strategic developments of the late 1960s to suggest that either Britain or France will be forced for strategic or technological reasons to abandon their own nuclear weapons programmes in the 1970s, though they may become more expensive to maintain, their credibility or political utility may be disputed, and they may incur the increasing disapproval of other countries. Our second assumption is that the present situation of nuclear inequality in Europe, as between the nuclear and non-nuclear states and as between small European nuclear forces and those of the super-powers, will persist unless European governments take a conscious decision to rectify both disparities (see especially Chapter Six, pp. 133–8).

How active will the Western Europe of the 1970s be in trying to influence developments outside the industrial world, in Africa, Asia, or Latin America? The answer ought, perhaps, to be that there can be no enduring form of European political association that does not take account of the importance of the Third World, and that does not envisage Europe playing an important role in minimizing conflict or promoting development there. The European powers are all, with the exception of the two Germanies and Switzerland, members of the UN, and are bound by its obligations; it is unrealistic to expect that Europe can remain insulated from conflict elsewhere indefinitely, especially if it engages the interests of the super-powers; and the ex-colonial powers which number six out of the ten possible members of an enlarged Community, feel varying degrees of responsibility towards their former possessions.

Yet there are four reasons for assuming that Western Europe's preoccupations will be largely Eurocentric in the

1970s. In the first place, the drama of the unfolding relationship between Eastern and Western Europe is going to occupy a great deal of the attention of both governments and public opinion. For that matter, in certain of the models we have sketched, particularly the two variants of a Federal Europe, so would the drama of a new political structure in Western Europe itself. Second, there are now few illusions in European governments that an active and united European policy in the developing world would be accepted or would be influential in averting conflict, a disillusionment which the American failure in Vietnam has tended to substantiate. Third, the link between conflict in the developing world and the level of tension in Europe is now regarded as tenuous, always with the exception of conflict in the Middle East where European economic interests are involved and security interests could be involved. This does not mean that there could not be a co-ordinated single and expanded European policy on development aid, or might not have to be a closely co-ordinated policy on the sale of armaments to the developing countries.

The final reason why the impetus for most forms of European association in the 1970s is likely to be related to European rather than global considerations is that to proceed with more ambitious objectives in mind is likely to arouse such a diversity of views and interests as to make the job of European construction much harder. It would be difficult enough, for instance, to construct any form of European defence organization for purposes of European security alone, without suggesting, in addition that its forces could be used in, say, the Indian Ocean or Africa. From this follows our third assumption that Western Europe's relations with the developing world will be of secondary importance in determining the choices it must make about the structure of its internal association.

It is very probable that the Warsaw Pact will undergo marked changes in the 1970s. Several of its members chafe under the highly centralized system of military command and control on which the Russians insist, or wish to have more political discussion and to use it as an instrument for influencing

Soviet policy. The Soviet Union will almost certainly have to accept some relaxation of control and discrimination in her treatment of her allies, if internal liberalization, economic reform and resentment of Soviet dominance are not to break up the system, whatever steps are taken to suppress or control them, and spread to countries crucial to the Pact's functions as a security instrument, namely Poland and East Germany. East Germany after Ulbricht, perhaps in the course of rapprochement between the two Germanies, may follow her neighbours in adopting a more independent position *vis-à-vis* Moscow. But as long as the Soviet Union remains the sole source not only of strategic protection for Eastern Europe but also of conventional arms for local deterrence, as long as Eastern European countries feel that they have a more serious security problem *vis-à-vis* Western Europe than *vis-à-vis* each other, it is our assumption that the multilateral pact is unlikely to be dissolved, even though some countries, especially in the Southern tier, may have a looser relationship with it.

There is no sign of the Soviet Union abandoning her basic conviction that her strategic frontier is on the Elbe and that her security requires a capacity to hold Western Europe hostage, should a crisis arise in which she wished to induce American caution; nor would a Soviet–American dialogue on restraint in strategic forces necessarily prompt a change of attitude. Furthermore, the Soviet Union will feel more gradually the economic pressures which in the West are rapidly making defence less cost-effective and causing NATO members anxiously to seek reductions in their forces in Europe. But as her own strategic position in relation to the United States improves, Western Europe's hostage value will become less significant, while technological developments will continue to undermine the value of Eastern Europe as a defensive *glacis*. The possibility of some Soviet reduction of forces in East Germany in, say, five years' time should not therefore be excluded. But we assume that there need be no marked reductions in the early 1970s in the forces which the Soviet Union maintains in Central Europe.

12

If the Warsaw Pact seems likely to endure through the next decade, even though its internal structure may be modified and the level of forces at its disposal reduced, so also does the Atlantic Alliance. It is true that there have been powerful pressures working for a modification in the level of forces which the United States maintains in Europe. Though it is reasonable to assume that the American military commitment in Vietnam will have been liquidated by the mid-1970s, and is unlikely to be transferred to other potential trouble spots on the Asian mainland, such as Thailand, it is clear that the United States will still have to maintain an active offshore military presence in the Pacific. As the problems of domestic policy, urban renewal, rural poverty, public health, education and welfare, make new demands on the federal budget, there will be pressures to divert resources from defence. Since few economies will be possible in expenditure on strategic systems – even if some agreement with the Soviet Union keeps the cost from rising sharply – it is in the 250,000 American troops deployed in Europe that Congress is likely to demand economies. At the same time the development of the C-5A, the 500-man long-range troop carrier, which will be ready in the early 1970s, will make it possible for the United States to argue that she can maintain at home, say, three of the five divisions which she now deploys in Germany, and still redeploy them there during the period of strategic warning which would, so it is argued, precede a European crisis. Similarly tactical air units can, with flight refuelling, re-cross the Atlantic in a short time. Although the European members of NATO are still sceptical of the military and political implications of a long-range reinforcement capability of this kind, and feel that it is an inadequate substitute for American forces permanently deployed in Central Europe and familiar with the terrain, they are resigning themselves to the fact that it will be put into operation by the new administration in due course. But, most West European governments will want to maintain a multilateral political and security relationship with the United States. Moreover, the European members of NATO will be loth to accept any modification in its structure which appears seriously to weaken the American commitment, such as the replacement of an American Supreme Commander by a European. Some of the models explore the implications for NATO of different kinds of European association, including the possibility of its disruption. But however disenchanted opinion in the United States may be with the political rewards of her twenty-year guardianship of European security, in terms of allied support for her Asian policies or affection for her society; however insupportable relatively secure countries like France may find American domination of the alliance; however distasteful it may be to the student generation in Europe; the governments, and main political parties, of the more exposed countries in Europe will respond with considerable reluctance to the prospect of alterations in the present alliance system so drastic as to seem to weaken the American strategic commitment.

Thus our six basic assumptions are that, *other things being equal*, the central balance of power will remain basically bipolar; that the present disparity between nuclear and non-nuclear states in Western Europe will persist unless the situation is altered by an explicit political act; that the structure of Western Europe will not be significantly affected by conflict or developments in the Third World; that the countries of Eastern Europe will not be anxious to abrogate the Warsaw Pact whatever their differences with Moscow; that the Soviet Union will become only gradually reconciled to the withdrawal of forces from Central Europe; and that most West European powers will acquiesce in a substantial withdrawal of American forces, but will be anxious to maintain NATO in some form. Our models, however, examine variations in all these norms.

These assumptions may be criticized for being too conservative, or for being at variance with the restless temper of the younger generation in Europe. They are, however, consistent with the observable attitudes of contemporary governments. Moreover, there is in Western Europe in the late 1960s, a detectable swing in favour of politically conservative parties or governments, though conservatism in domestic politics does not necessarily imply a conservative attitude to new forms of international association. The conservative temper of West European governments in the late 1960s and early 1970s and the slowness with which governments change their positions on issues like security or sovereignty, when combined with the desire for change in the coming generation, suggests two points which form our final assumptions: first, that there will be more debate than action in the early 1970s: second, that thereafter, as the post-war generation enters the corridors of power, the pace of political and international change will accelerate.

## IV

The technique of model-building, as a device for eliciting the underlying implications in a complex series of interactions and relationships, is one well established in the social sciences. It can be used either to develop a conceptual framework for the refinement of political or economic theory, or as a means of illuminating the connotations of choices which confront the policy-maker. It is for this second purpose that ISS decided to cast its current contribution to the debate on the future of Western Europe in the form of six models of the structure of association that *could* develop there during the next decade.

We must, however, make certain reservations about the value of this method, and about our own approach in particular. First, the building of models may clarify the implications of political and economic choices, but it is not, as Professor Bell has said, a form of prediction. Though we have developed six alternative structures of Western Europe in the 1970s which would be logically consistent with the dominance of different combinations of motives and pressures, it is certain that the European entity which eventually emerges will not correspond precisely to any of them, and may indeed be an amalgam of several.

For one thing, the small group of Europeans which has constructed the models is fallible, and may not have succeeded in comprehending and reflecting the full range of European objectives, desires or ingenuity. But there is a more fundamental limitation to model-building as a technique for depicting the future: it cannot successfully take account of the element of chance in human affairs, the incidence of war, economic or social catastrophe, or the emergence of powerful idiosyncratic leaders. No study of Europe in the 1960s published ten years ago could have foreseen the influence of President de Gaulle on European affairs, or the expansion of the Vietnam conflict into a war and its influence upon European–American relations. Moreover, it is impossible to predict the clash of circumstance and personality which may modify the evolution of an international structure such as any sketched in this book.

This general reservation has governed our approach and led us to adopt certain rules and limitations which should be made explicit.

(1) We have not attempted to devise details of the particular train of events or combination of circumstances which may lead to the construction of a particular form of association in Western Europe. We have, however, attempted in this chapter to estimate the principal forces in international politics in the 1970s, that will form the background of Europe's choices.

(2) We have constructed our models around the countries of Western Europe, and only then have we examined the effect of each model on Western Europe's relations with the United States, the Soviet Union, Eastern Europe and the developing world. This, of course, assumes that Western Europe controls its own destiny to a greater extent than may be the case. It does not follow that we consider Western Europe a permanently self-contained entity, separate from Eastern Europe, or that we do not recognize the growing interdependence of Eastern and Western policies. This, too, has been done deliberately to emphasize the implications of the basic choices which confront Western Europe.

One limitation of our approach is that we do not examine

possible pan-European structures such as an association of EEC and COMECON or a European security system. But, having initiated various research studies on the latter a year or more ago, we are impressed with the difficulty of putting any flesh on various skeleton concepts of a European security system until there are clearer indications of how the political and military structure of Western Europe will develop.[3]

(3) In the European models we offer for inspection in this study not all the concomitant innovations in political, economic and defence arrangements have been explored. We have tried to concentrate on what has seemed to us the most significant aspects of each model and, given the interests of ISS, have emphasized the security aspects more than the economic or sociological. Our comments in the chapters on the various models have been confined primarily to the internal consistency, and therefore feasibility, of each model in order to provide a basis for comparison of their relative strengths and weaknesses. At the risk of repetition, it is to clarify Europe's choices, to elicit at least the outlines of the stresses and strains, the opportunities and risks, which progression in a particular direction involves, that we have chosen this particular approach. While no one of the models may seem, by itself, satisfactory, in Chapter seven we have tried to compare the implications of each choice and, by evaluating their merits and relative probabilities, to extract what might prove to be a realistic and promising answer to Europe's problems in the next decade.

(4) It may be asked why, in view of the uncertainties, we have not examined a broader range of alternatives, such as an alliance between the Soviet Union and Western Europe or its leading powers, or some radical revision of international alignments, such as an organic union of the English-speaking countries. The answer is that these six models have been winnowed

[3] This was one of the conclusions reached in the first ISS study on the subject, Alastair Buchan and Philip Windsor, *Arms and Stability in Europe* (London: Chatto and Windus, 1963), and is implicit in the latest one, Pierre Hassner, *Change and Security in Europe*, Parts I and II, Adelphi Papers 45 and 49 (London: ISS, 1968).

from a much wider range of theoretical alternatives, and have been defined by our own conviction that the risks of structural innovation for a group of powers which forms one element in a delicate global balance mean that Western Europe's freedom of choice is limited.

(5) We have confined our examination to the next decade in the full knowledge that a more adventurous range of possibilities for Europe can be envisaged if one casts one's imagination up to and beyond the beginning of the next century, as Herman Kahn and other futurologists have attempted to do.[4] Certainly one must bear in mind the possible developments of the 1980s, especially in the field of science and technology, if one is to make any comment on the political choices of the 1970s. But much long-range political and economic prediction is mere speculation on slender evidence, and it seems to us that it is in the next decade that the West European powers, whether they are to fragment or cohere, have to make the decisions which will determine much of the pattern of international politics in the 1980s and 1990s.

We may be open to the opposite charge of having telescoped the course of future events. Perhaps some of the alternative relationships which we sketch can hardly be expected to mature in so short a period of time. But the basic decisions and the re-examination of national interests on which they must be based can hardly be deferred beyond the next decade.

[4] See Kahn and Wiener, *The Year 2,000*, or 'Towards the Year 2,000: Work in Progress', *Daedalus*, Summer 1967.

Chapter One

# EVOLUTIONARY EUROPE

I

The countries of Western Europe, as this study assumes, are masters of their destiny; they can either take a step forward and establish a new political structure, or they can remain largely passive. *Evolutionary Europe* is a passive choice.

However, this passivity does not stem from a loss of faith in 'the European idea'. The West European governments remain officially committed to some form of political union as an ultimate goal, though they may disagree on what form it should take. But they do not regard it as being attainable in the foreseeable future, and are too concerned with individual, short-term difficulties to spare much energy for discussion let alone common action. The Benelux countries, Italy, Britain and Germany, may in principle all favour a close West European union in partnership with the United States. But Britain is preoccupied with her economic problems. Germany, having seen her post-war hopes of European integration disappointed, is reluctant to launch a new initiative, more especially since this might conflict with her Eastern Policy. France, aiming at a loose European coalition and independence from both superpowers, gives priority to building up her national economic, strategic and diplomatic position. The Scandinavian countries, though attracted by the European idea, prefer to wait until the course of events in Europe becomes clearer before they commit themselves fully.

In short, there is no sign of a *relance européenne*. European integration is no longer at the top of the agenda for any European government. More important, governments fear that its serious consideration would bring their divergence of views about political union into open controversy and cause a split between them, that could jeopardize the European idea altogether. They prefer to let the question rest and wait for better times.[1] Western Europe becomes too preoccupied with the problems of today to spare time for those of tomorrow.


## II


The structure of Western Europe remains basically the same as it is today. The European communities, EEC, ECSC, and Euratom, proceed towards economic union, but progress is slow. The Community advances in what John Pinder has called 'negative integration', that is, the removal of discrimination.[2] The Community administers the common external tariff of the customs union and non-tariff barriers inside the union are gradually abolished. The obstacles to the free movement of labour, services and capital are removed and further safeguards against unequal competition are created by introducing a uniform tax system and company law.

The member states of the community in the 1970s find these steps of negative integration compatible with their general reluctance to embark upon any form of political union. The removal of discrimination prejudices neither Europe's ultimate political structures nor the way in which governments are to organize their co-operation. But the member states are reluctant to go beyond that stage and develop 'positive integration', a process designed not merely to remove discrimination but to reshape economic and social policy on a common basis. In *Evolutionary Europe* there is no common monetary policy, no

---

[1] Herr Brandt said in a speech on 4 May 1968: 'In view of existing differences of opinion – even though it is not always easy to sympathize with another viewpoint – we must first acknowledge that there is still no unanimity on what is good and right for Europe or even how this Europe should be created. The German Government is convinced, however, that what is necessary for Europe will gain the upper hand in the long run, despite all the difficulties and an occasional critical phase.'

[2] See 'Positive and Negative Integration, Some Problems of Economic Union in EEC', *The World Today*, March 1968.

co-ordinated technological policy, and only limited steps towards a common commercial policy.

The euphoria of the early 1960s, when the success of the European Economic Community seemed to promise rapid progress towards political integration, has subsided, but so also has the opposition to new members. Since the Common Market has been shorn of political aspirations, applications are judged solely in economic terms. Britain, her economy gradually acquiring dynamism and stability again, leads Norway, Denmark and Ireland into the Communities. This, however, has the effect of further slowing down the process of integration. 'The Community institutions are already cumbersome and slow-moving, and simply adding new members, however European-minded they may be, adds to the difficulties.'[3]

The other collective structure in Europe, NATO, remains unchanged. France sees no reason for returning to it, though she remains a member of the Atlantic Alliance, but her absence from the integrated military and political machinery does not, as was once hoped, facilitate closer co-operation between the remaining members of the organization. It is not enthusiasm for an integrated defence organization that prevents other West European states from following her example, but rather the absence of anything to take NATO's place as a basis for their security. West European governments, in varying degrees, become less concerned about security, and their defence budgets come under increasing scrutiny. American troops remain in Europe, but are reduced to less than 100,000 men, on the ground that the introduction of strategic transport allows for a rapid return of American troops to Europe in a crisis. But on the whole West European governments tend to discount the danger of a military confrontation in Central Europe and to emphasize NATO's role as first an instrument of *détente* which may, together with the Warsaw Pact, provide the framework of an eventual European security system, and second, a political means of keeping tuned in to the Soviet–American dialogue.

[3] Miriam Camps, *European Unification in the Sixties* (New York and London: McGraw-Hill, 1966), p. 220.

But again, none of them, with the exception of France, is prepared to take the full risk of exploiting a situation of *détente*. They want to remain assured of American protection, but, at the same time, are reluctant to accept a greater share of the burdens of the Alliance. They are afraid of becoming too closely linked to American policy objectives, but are not prepared to work openly for European independence.

But European governments in the 1970s find that they cannot afford to maintain an entirely passive attitude to co-operation if they are not to run the risk of becoming technologically and industrially backward. Technological and industrial considerations exert increasing influence on European political attitudes, and the belief that economic growth and technological efforts are interdependent is widely supported, while American prowess is widely, if irrationally, resented. But governments in Western Europe realize that they cannot meet the requirements of technological growth nor answer the 'American challenge' on a purely national basis. Co-operation on a bilateral and even multilateral basis is accepted as the logical solution to this dilemma if Europe's more limited resources of skills are to be employed effectively. Frequent consultations on this matter continue to be held by governments within the frame-work of the Council of Ministers of the European Communities and outside it. Yet governments are afraid of their own logic. Agreement is limited to inter-governmental co-operation which is not intended to provide a comprehensive European policy for science and technology but simply to provide a clearing-house to encourage *ad hoc* coalitions for specific bilateral or multilateral projects. Similar trends of inter-governmental co-operation are developed in the field of computers and nuclear energy. After the disappointing experience of the European Launcher Development Organization no attempt is made to revive a European space programme, though the European Space Research Organization continues as a research centre. The European Commission is not endowed with power to co-ordinate research or to encourage industrial joint ventures.

New impulses towards co-operation are also felt in the field of defence. Though security considerations are no longer paramount, economic necessity demands a new collective effort. As the price of modern equipment continues to rise, especially in high-technology products, the only way governments can make ends meet, once they have exhausted the possibilities of manpower reduction, is by pooling research and development resources, pushing forward the standardization of weapons and decreasing unit costs by providing a larger market.[4] The United States still has the potential to dominate the European arms market; the great American aviation and electronics companies, geared to large-scale production and massively supported in their sales drive by their government, present a constant temptation to West European governments to buy American at the expense of European industries.[5] These governments face the alternatives of either succumbing to this temptation or making their own defence industries more competitive by pooling their resources. Willy-nilly they chose the second, realizing that the alternative to increasing dependence on each other may be total dependence on the United States, both in defence and in civil high, technology products.

This leads to the establishment of a West European arms procurement group within NATO, a European Defence Committee.[6] It is not a supra-national agency and is not conceived as the nucleus of a European Defence Community on the pattern

[4] Between 1963 and 1968 the cost of military equipment in Britain was expected to rise at the following rate: tank battalion $+100$ per cent, artillery battalion $+300$ per cent, infantry battalion $+600$ per cent, light aircraft $=500$ per cent, sea-to-air missiles $+700$ per cent. See *Statement on British Defence Estimates 1965*, p. 6. The increases in unit costs in the early 1970s are not, however, as dramatic as in the 1960s.

[5] In 1965 the United States Department of Defence projected arms sales of about $1.5 billion per year between 1965 and 1975. (This is about one fifth of the total West European arms procurement.) C. J. E. Harlow, *Defence, Technology and the Western Alliance*, No. 2, *The European Armaments Base: A Survey, Part 1* (London: ISS, 1967), p. 31.

[6] For a more elaborate institutional form of European Defence, the European Defence Community, see chapter Five (*Partnership Europe*).

envisaged in 1952. It is a formalized West European caucus within NATO, whose main participants are Britain, Germany, Italy, Belgium and Holland. It is an intergovernmental body, intended to co-ordinate weapons requirements, and to facilitate *ad hoc* co-operative projects and, perhaps, at a later stage, joint defence planning. But governments are careful to provide for flexible arrangements that do not exclude projects involving outsiders, France, Sweden or the United States. They are cautious about becoming irrevocably committed to joint ventures, and they are anxious to keep the door open for withdrawal from joint procurement projects should their national interests demand it.

While West European governments may submit to the pressures created by technological progress they also resent them and are unwilling to accept their full implications. They avoid the creation of new forms of international organization and are only reluctantly drawn into adaptations of old ones. Anxious that others should not relinquish existing commitments, they are unwilling to assume fresh responsibilities themselves. This may be a safe attitude to pursue in the 1970s; and it may be true that Western Europe's best choice is to wait and see, hoping for a better opportunity to solve her problems. But might she not have lost her options by the time that opportunity arrives?

## III

With this structure, the states of *Evolutionary Europe* will sooner or later have to face the fact that they cannot indefinitely keep open the options implicit in the various concepts of European political union: the option between independence from and dependence on the United States, between a loose European concert and a European federation, between a wider Europe including Eastern Europe, and a purely Western Europe of the Common Market, even if enlarged.

Negative integration within the European Communities, however advantageous for the economies of its member states, will not be sufficient to put Western Europe on a common economic basis. Nor will it enable it to wield the influence in international trade that a unified entity might enjoy. A half-way economic union will make the member states individually subject to pressures from third countries exploiting the lack of unity and trying to play off one member state against another – an incomplete economic union would provide member states with less individual power than they had had before and less collective power than they would have once the union was completed. Member states may realize this, but, having lost faith in European union as a goal that can be attained in the foreseeable future, they may try to overcome the shortcomings by greater emphasis on national policy, thus weakening further such collective structures as exist.

This tendency will be particularly evident in the field of technology. The 'technological gap', superiority of American to European high-technology industries and the fear of European dependence, will be an important political issue in Western Europe of the 1970s, even if the problem of American investment may have acquired less disquieting proportions than developments in the early 1960s seemed to indicate. Negative economic integration offers a particularly favourable opportunity to American firms in Europe as it provides a large market but stops short of a common industrial policy that could effectively encourage the development of large-scale European industries. As Christopher Layton has pointed out, even a policy of mergers, designed to encourage the creation of European companies to match the size of their American competitors, would need to be backed by other positive policies: 'More and better management training, more information of company accounts to ensure that mergers and take-overs are judicious, lower interest rates and economic policies which encourage investment, all these things form part of the climate that must be created if European industry is to respond as vigorously as possible to the American challenge and to adapt itself to the opportunities of the Common Market.'[7] Without a determined common European policy this objective cannot be reached.

The steps *Evolutionary Europe* is willing to take do not exclude some progress towards solving the peripheral problems – a common company law, a common patent law and the facilitation of industrial mergers across national borders. But Europe will be in a weak position at a time when economic growth is increasingly linked to efficient technological investment, and when Europe's position in the industrial world and the attraction it exerts on Eastern Europe and the developing countries is conditioned by what it can offer, in competition with the United States, the Soviet Union and Japan, in the technological field.

Not even in joint defence procurement, which would seem the most obvious field for initial steps in European technological co-operation, does *Evolutionary Europe* offer bright prospects. Joint procurement and, possibly, joint production of weapons are both the most obvious and the most difficult areas for common efforts. It is the most obvious field of co-operation because governments are disposed to allocate considerable resources of money and skill, and because, in Western Europe, all of them realize that they cannot afford a purely national arms production base. However, joint defence procurement faces the most formidable obstacles which will discourage the cautious governments of *Evolutionary Europe*. As they are not prepared to hand over responsibility to a European authority of the Community type, endowed with a long-term budget and the power to stimulate research and development and to co-ordinate national programmes, they will run into all the snags that have characterized intergovernmental co-operation in this field in the 1960s: a long lapse of time from the instigation of the original project to production, constant uncertainty about costs and economic viability that tempts governments to opt out of the common effort, and the vicious circle of the *juste retour* – all govern-

[7] Christopher Layton, *Trans-Atlantic Investments*. The Atlantic Papers (Paris: Atlantic Institute, 1966), p. 75.

ments wanting to recoup their investment in orders for their own industries.[8]

The other major difficulty is less economic than political. For joint arms procurement to work, the views of participant governments on the military requirements of weapons must be if not identical, at least co-ordinated. This need for co-ordination of defence policies may not arise with simpler forms of equipment, but the more complex the weapons system, the less it is able to span diverging operational requirements. Thus joint defence planning and joint decision-making must precede joint procurement. Rhodes James has pointed out that for joint procurement within NATO to be successful it is essential that the Alliance determine its military strategy and material priorities; it is essential that it decide what kind of war it is likely to become involved in as an alliance, and this applies to any endeavour of joint arms procurement, particularly if research is entailed.[9] The co-ordination of defence-related research as well as long-term purchasing commitments implies a degree of mutual confidence and wholehearted acceptance of interdependence that is only possible if the participating governments agree not only in principle on the nature of future threats to their security, but in considerable detail on how to deter or react to them. It also requires basic agreement on whether European weapons should be sold to countries in the developing world, for example, Israel, the Arab states and South Africa, and if so, to whom and in what proportions. Because governments in *Evolutionary Europe* are unlikely to gain this confidence or have the courage to overcome the many difficulties, there can be no successful programmes of joint development in weapons or civil high technology in Western Europe. Instead the bigger countries may try to increase their national

---

[8] See Malcolm W. Hoag, *Defence Economics in Action in America* (Santa Monica: Rand Corporation, March 1968), p. 8.

[9] For a full account see *Defence Technology and the Western Alliance*, No. 3, *Standardization and Common Production of Weapons in NATO* by Robert Rhodes James, and No. 6, *The Implications of a European System for Defence Technology* by Alastair Buchan, pp. 15–16.

armaments base, occasionally entering bilateral arrangements on the pattern of the Anglo-French aviation projects of the 1960s, while the smaller and industrially weaker countries continue to buy American weapons. The example of defence procurement applies in general to co-operation in high technology. The technological challenge does not, in *Evolutionary Europe*, cause greater unity but, by the inefficiency of half-hearted international co-operation, encourages national cartels and thereby increases disintegration.

The justification for this Europe is that it provides for efficient handling of short-term problems, in anticipation of a time more propitious for building a political community, but the European governments may discover too late that opportunities do not present themselves unaided. They will find their economies largely dependent on American money, innovation and management. For the possible political consequences of these developments see Chapter Two (*Atlanticized Europe*). They will find their defence co-operation dissolving with the Alliance a development which might not threaten their security, but would certainly lower Western Europe's diplomatic standing in the eyes of the Soviet Union and Eastern Europe, and create the danger of imbalance that Europe itself will lack the power to redress. Nor will political union survive as a viable aim in this kind of Europe. Public opinion will weary of it as it seems to be increasingly contradicted by reality, and will soon be tired even of lip-service to it. At best, this idea may serve as an excuse for purely national policies – national science policy, national economic policy, national defence policy will be declared to be in the interest of Europe. There will be in fact a polarization of individual interests at the expense of the collective interest. Domestic issues will return to the forefront of political debate in Western Europe as foreign policy considerations cease to command the attention accorded them during the Cold War years. Education and welfare, urban problems of individual nations, and the adjustment of outdated political systems to the requirements of post-industrial societies, will become the objects of the best energies of governments and the expectations of public opinion. Little will remain as a basis for far-reaching collective initiatives in Europe.

## IV

Whatever the specific relations between this Europe and other nations or groups of nations, three general observations seem to apply.

First, *Evolutionary Europe* is a diplomatically weak Europe. While in some specialized matters, e.g. negotiations such as those of the Kennedy Round, Western Europe may speak with one voice, as a rule it will lack the political cohesion to do so. Or so it will appear to its negotiating partners. Even if the governments do from time to time establish a common position, they may be unable to withstand their opponents' attempts to divide them.

Second, *Evolutionary Europe* invites interference by other powers. It is a Europe groping its way, unsure where it is going. Outside powers, especially the super-powers with their high stake in the European balance of power, will try to persuade this Western Europe to take the direction most suited to their own objectives.

Third, and this is a consequence of both the preceding observations, *Evolutionary Europe* can be treated as an entity in international relations only in a very limited sense. The foreign policy implications of this model are felt differently by the different member countries, as it favours some at the expense of others. *Evolutionary Europe* may not be an advantageous formula for Europe as such, but this is not necessarily true for the individual countries.

What are the specific implications of *Evolutionary Europe* for the Atlantic relationship and for East–West relations in Europe? For the United States, *Evolutionary Europe* would be economically attractive but politically irritating. Economic benefits, already considerable in the Europe of today, are likely to continue as Europe grows into a common market.

Negative economic integration, in abolishing discrimination, will, in fact, discriminate in favour of the American subsidiaries in Western Europe as they are generally better equipped to reap the advantages of a large market than are European firms. Economic interdependence, both of Europe in relation to the United States and of the United States in relation to Europe, will grow in *Evolutionary Europe*. But the nature of the relationship will be determined by the United States. Western Europe, without a common objective, or at least, without the common will to work for one, will be able only to react, in spite of its importance as a trading partner, to the United States and its role in the international monetary system. At best, Western Europe could block undesired American measures, but there would be no basis from which the relationship could be developed into a common European–American position.

*Evolutionary Europe's* reluctance to be too firmly linked to the United States will become less and less consistent with economic reality. Against its inclination Europe will find itself moving towards Atlanticization. Political relations between Western Europe and the United States will be affected by this development. The anti-Americanism emerging in the late 1960s is, to a considerable extent, a product of European resentment of American economic and technological penetration. In the 1970s, when industrial and technological considerations may be even more important, this resentment is likely to increase. It will be readily exploited by a coalition of nationalist movements and old Europeanists who blame the United States, or American capitalism, for the political divisions of Europe and its inertia in overcoming them.

Europe will present scant opportunity for the United States to put the political relationship on a sounder basis. American political leaders, though irritated by the process of alienation they witness in Europe, will feel unable to stop it. They will continue to support the timid efforts of West European collective organizations in the field of technological co-operation and defence. But given these organizations' probable inefficiency, the United States will only pay lip-service to the traditional concept of partnership, and proceed to reassess her relations with Europe. The 'Grand Design' will no longer be considered the formula for American relations with Europe best suited to the interests of the United States. Instead it will be recognized that, in the political and military contexts, the Europe most suited to American interests would be a 'Europe, including Britain, insufficiently united to reach for nuclear autonomy but still unified enough to go some way towards meeting the European desire for political identity and independence, while, at the same time, restricting German and French freedom of action considerably'.[10] The United States has too much at stake, economically and politically, simply to opt out of European affairs. Even though she will be able to withdraw from the Atlantic Alliance at one year's notice, she will be aware that an important aspect of the central balance of power in the world would collapse if she did so, and she will in any case remain bound by strong ties of friendship and loyalty not only to the larger but also to the smaller countries of Western Europe. She must therefore try and maintain as strong a political position in Europe as she can.

Her policy will, therefore, be to strengthen relations with her closest post-war allies, Germany and Britain, rather than to try breathing new life into a revised concept of European–American partnership. This approach, however damaging to what little West European cohesion remains, is unlikely to be spurned by the two countries in question. Britain, though now a member of the Common Market and content with a role in Europe more restricted than any she has played for a long time, could be induced to commit her interests to the reliable American ally rather than cast her lot entirely with the casual and unpromising *Evolutionary Europe*. Germany will still be too much aware of her dependence for security on American support to reject a 'special relationship'. The more she is concerned with security, the more she will be prepared to sacrifice

[10] Harold van B. Cleveland, *The Atlantic Idea and its European Rivals* (New York and London: McGraw-Hill, 1966), p. 163.

her hopes of a change of the *status quo* in Central Europe for American support. It is in this respect that American and Soviet interests would not be dissimilar. Both super-powers would, for different reasons, want the *status quo* in Europe to continue; both would regard the pursuit by Bonn of a dynamic policy of *détente* as liable to affect their position in Europe adversely, the Soviet Union fearing an erosion of her control over Eastern Europe and the United States a German–Soviet rapprochement.[11] While in a united Europe the reunification of Germany would be considered advantageous to American policies, in a bilateral relationship the *status quo* would serve American interests better.

A Western Europe which can achieve only inter-governmental co-operation and which hesitates to go further would have little direct influence upon the Soviet Union, nor would it cause her to revise her view that, in Europe if not elsewhere, she continues to possess considerable diplomatic freedom of manœuvre. Her interest is, as Pierre Hassner has said, 'to obtain acceptance of the Eastern and German *status quo* and at the same time to encourage in the West divisions which could give the Soviet Union the choice between a broader *entente* with the United States and an anti-American *entente* with the Europeans'.[12] *Evolutionary Europe* would give her the opportunity to maintain that interest by an adroit policy which stopped short of any form of *promenade militaire* that might shock Western Europe either into real unity or into a revitalized security and political relationship with the United States.

She could, for instance, develop an intimate dialogue with the United States on problems of global strategy, which would tend to arouse European suspicions, and simultaneously draw the main West European powers, except Germany, into discussion of purely European security arrangements, to which they might be attracted by their desire to increase contacts with

[11] See George W. Ball, *The Discipline of Power* (London: Bodley Head; Boston: Atlantic-Little, Brown, 1968), p. 166.

[12] Pierre Hassner, *Change and Security in Europe*, Part I, Adelphi Paper 45 (London: ISS, 1968), p. 17.

Eastern Europe. If so, they would find their commitment to Germany's aim of reunification an increasing hindrance to their discussions with the Soviet Union which could insist on acceptance of the territorial *status quo* as the basis of any progress on arms control or security. The Soviet Union would, thus, present Germany with a range of difficult choices: seeking a West European political arrangement stronger than mere *entente* and involving integration of European foreign policies; demanding American support for her position: opening independent negotiations with the Soviet Union. But it might be too late to accomplish the first. There is no certainty that the United States could still make her delicate global negotiations with the Soviet Union dependent on Soviet acceptance of a settlement of the German problem, even though she might continue formally to support it. And the third alternative, direct German negotiations with Moscow, carries no certainty of success, given the disparity in the power of the two countries. Consequently, while Germany might obtain from *Evolutionary Europe* a certain latitude in re-establishing relations with Eastern Europe, the Soviet Union could evolve from it a diplomatic situation that left Germany isolated from her Western neighbours, without risking a degree of tension that would have a really cohesive effect on Western Europe or rally it under American leadership. Moreover, in such a Europe the Soviet Union can use Berlin so as to exert pressure at a level that affects German interests more than those of the three Allied powers.[13]

Friction would inevitably arise within a Western Europe that could achieve only inter-governmental co-operation. Such limited co-operation in defence matters would not greatly concern the Soviet Union – particularly a Soviet Union that was approaching or had reached strategic parity with the United States. But she would certainly attempt to exploit any form of

[13] This possibility was illustrated in mid-June 1968 when East Germany imposed on West German citizens a special visa and an increased transit tax for travel to and from West Berlin via East German territory. The Western allies in their protest notes objected less to the restrictive measures introduced than to the nature of their justification.

European defence co-operation and the German role in it, to weaken relations between Eastern and Western Europe, and strengthen the Warsaw Pact.

But a politically passive Western Europe does offer certain advantages in broader relations with Eastern Europe. Devoid of political dynamism, it would not challenge Soviet political control over Eastern Europe or justify greater domination by them. This would give the East European countries time in which to diversify their economies and gradually lessen their economic dependence on the Soviet Union. Since the EEC is no more than an economic arrangement, they can also co-operate according to need with any individual West European country without fear that entering a close trading relationship will eventually be put to political purpose or turned to their political disadvantage. Eastern Europe might be particularly attracted to the establishment of lines with West European technological industries and to the prospect of obtaining Western plant or know-how. Increased American penetration of West European markets would not really affect this issue, for the East Europeans will probably continue to regard Western Europe as their natural shopping centre for technological products regardless of whether the European supplier is an American subsidiary or not. Moreover, buying from Western Europe offers a possibility of getting access to American know-how without trading directly with the United States. The Soviet Union which has hitherto been able to insist that Eastern Europe purchase capital equipment mainly from her, on the ground that technological co-operation with Western Europe might carry a security risk, would find it harder to maintain that position. It is true that the Soviet handling of Czechoslovakia in 1968 revealed an apprehension that a gradual increase in trade and technological co-operation between the states of Eastern Europe and Western Europe might lead to a loosening of the Warsaw Pact, and indicated that she still desires the economic dependence of her satellites almost as much as on political control. But this hard line may have to be gradually adjusted as economic reform and adjustment to international competition continue to be major problems for all of Eastern Europe.

Thus, despite the fact that a politically passive Western Europe offers not a few diplomatic advantages to the Soviet Union, it also carries – provided the West European states remain economically dynamic – certain longer term diplomatic risks. *Evolutionary Europe* is by no means pure gain for Moscow.

## V

*Evolutionary Europe's* structure and its impact on external relations can be summed up as follows: no political cohesion among West European states, no efforts to bring it about; the United States remains politically and militarily present in Europe. There is no radical change, but a greater diversity in East–West relations as the policies of West European countries are no longer governed by a common approach.

What are the impacts of *Evolutionary Europe* on the major West European countries? At first sight, it looks as if Germany should be ranged among the prime losers, as the model offers neither a solution to her national problem nor compensation by way of an influential position within a West European political structure. However, this assessment depends on what Germany will regard as her most important foreign policy objective in the 1970s. While *Evolutionary Europe* excludes outright reunification, it leaves open the 'indirect approach' of *détente* with Eastern Europe and rapprochement between the two German states. It does not, however, promise easy success even for this more modest political aim. There are no signs that the Soviet Union would readily tolerate increased West German political activity in that area or rapprochement with East Germany. Soviet policy would rather be to discourage Germany – and other Western states – from what she would regard as meddling in her sphere of influence.

She would be supported in this attitude by East German

leaders, increasingly nervous not only that the virus of liberalization in other East European countries might infect their own subjects, but also that a normalization of inter-European relations might leave East Germany isolated and even make the Soviet Union reluctant to remain committed to her. East Germany, aware of her economic and strategic importance to the Soviet Union, would do everything in her power to persuade the Soviet Union to maintain a rigid attitude towards West Germany. *Evolutionary Europe*, drained of political solidarity, would not provide sufficient support for Germany to survive a series of diplomatic reverses in her Eastern policy or to make her less susceptible to Soviet pressure. On the contrary, other West European governments might see advantages in bilateral agreements with the Soviet Union at the expense of Germany.

France would seem to be the most obvious winner in *Evolutionary Europe*. This model represents in many ways what she has been striving for in the 1960s: the loosening of the two alliance systems in Europe, as well as the reduction of American influence in Western and of Soviet influence in most of Eastern Europe. But France may not find this the best of all possible worlds. Her political role in both Eastern and Western Europe in the 1960s has derived from her ability to arrest the process of political union in Western Europe and to encourage independent policies in Eastern Europe. In the model of *Evolutionary Europe*, collective structures are disintegrating anyway, and France, having helped initiate this process, may lack the power to influence it. *Evolutionary Europe*, therefore, may be a disappointment for French foreign policy. France might be unacceptable to the West Europeans as a leader and to the super-powers as an interlocutor.

Those whose interests might suffer least in *Evolutionary Europe* will be those states which, neither by their political ambitions nor by their geographic position, threaten super-power interests. Britain and Italy could be in this category. Their relations with Eastern Europe, primarily economic, will flourish, and their very lack of political involvement will make them appear as acceptable mediators should Europe ever be ready to put its political and security relations on a new basis. However, these countries may be the most dissatisfied with the economic and technological inefficiency of *Evolutionary Europe*. Impatient with Europe's passivity, both may become the main promoters of a new European formula in the 1970s, just as Germany, France and Italy were in the 1950s.

To none of the major West European states does *Evolutionary Europe* offer a reasonable solution. It is an uncertain Western Europe: uncertain where it should go, how it should reorganize its internal structure, even doubtful if it should work for a collective structure at all. It is, at best, a transitory Europe.

Chapter Two

# ATLANTICIZED EUROPE

## I

In *Evolutionary Europe*, the West European states are passive, still trying to keep open the option of a political union but doubtful of each other and reluctant to become too closely committed to either of the super-powers. In *Atlanticized Europe*, they have renounced the aspiration of developing an independent system; they see their interests irrevocably linked to the United States and accept American leadership, though without enthusiasm.

One factor that makes subordination to American leadership Europe's choice is renewed concern about security, resulting from a European crisis, or a steady deterioration of Soviet-American relations, or simply the realization that *détente* relies on a fragile balance that can be upset by either design or mis-calculation – a tightening of Soviet control on Eastern Europe, or a flare-up of war in the Middle East causing a new confrontation between the super-powers. West European states, having reckoned on the continuation of *détente*, and accordingly reduced their defence efforts and accepted a certain degree of alienation from the United States, become anxiously aware of the limitations of independent West European policies. The security offered by American protection and its accompanying renunciation of independent European policies appears a sounder choice than the risks and dangers of *détente*.

There occurs, at the same time, a general reassessment of the role of West European powers in the framework of international politics as a whole. West European states have ceased to aspire to a united Europe capable of playing a significant part in world affairs. This is regarded as the special realm of the

38

existing super-powers who, by reason of their political and strategic power, their technological strength, the loyalties they can command and the resources they can mobilize, have moved into a category that is closed to any other country or group of countries. The effort of even trying to keep up with them is futile. West European states have but two alternatives: either to opt for a neutralist position, accepting their impotence and being at the mercy of both super-powers, or to accept a subordinate role in exchange for the protection of one of them. The United States, historically and culturally most closely related to Western Europe, is their ineluctable choice. The majority of West European states, with the possible exception of France, deliberately make that choice. Besides, in the post-war years, West Europeans have become accustomed to American leadership. Their attempts at setting up a political European union have been bedevilled by rivalries and mistrust. The leadership of one West European power is much less acceptable to the other West Europeans than American leadership.

Moreover, American leadership seems the key to economic and industrial progress, a consequence of the irrevocable process of American technological penetration of Europe and of growing economic interaction and interdependence among the industrialized Western states, in which American economic power, because of its size and dynamism, predominates.

The United States in the post-war years has forged far ahead of Europe in most areas of high technology that will be economically significant in the 1970s. The gap between Europe and America is constantly widening. As was prophesied in the late 1960s, the large market base, the superior capital resources, higher investment for research and development, as well as a broader education system and more efficient management methods, enable American industry to outbid European firms even in those markets where the latter still held a competitive position in the 1960s.[1] And though the inflow of American capital into Europe may have passed its peak, the position it

[1] Gerhard Stoltenberg, 'Die Zukunft als Forschungsgegenstand', *Frankfurther Allgemeine Zeitung*, 2 July 1968, p. 11.

has acquired during the 1950s and 1960s assures American firms of considerable influence on the European market.

West European firms, with a few exceptions, cease to challenge the American position and even invite the assistance of American capital, management and expertise in order to remain competitive. Governments, anxious to promote economic growth, welcome the inflow of American capital, endorsing the argument which has been used to point out the advantages for Britain of joining a North Atlantic Free Trade Area:

> While it is true that U.S. firms would tend to invest in Britain and would come to own a large part of British industry, this is not in itself a bad thing. One of the great obstacles to the growth of British economy and improvement in the British standard of living is lack of capital. American investment would be a new injection of capital which cannot but help increase our rate of growth.[2]

In *Atlanticized Europe*, American economic penetration is not only accepted, but considered essential for European welfare.

Moreover, the impetus to innovation in the field of high technology slackens in Europe; as European industries come to believe that they cannot win the technological race and catch up with American standards, they cease to try very hard.[3] And the prophecy of 1967 becomes a banality: 'Western Europe is in the process of becoming something close to a partial technological colony of the United States.'[4]

This European resignation to American superiority is made easier as governments realize that the state of their national economies is determined by the state of the economies of the community of industrialized countries as a whole, and that the degree of interaction and interdependence requires new international machinery to handle economic and monetary crises.

[2] Maxwell Stamp, 'The Atlantic Alternative to Europe', *Atlantic Community Quarterly*, Summer 1967, p. 188.
[3] See W. Haefele, 'The International Implications of Modern Technology', *NATO'S Fifteen Nations*, Vol. 12, No. 6, p. 64.
[4] William E. Griffiths, *The United States and the Soviet Union in Europe – the Impact of the Arms Race, Technology and the German Question* (Cambridge, Mass.: Massachusetts Institute of Technology, October 1967), p. 12.

Neither regional economic groupings like the EEC or EFTA, nor the United States can provide it on their own. It can only be established by joint co-operative efforts and who else but the United States, having minimized the economic burden of the Vietnam War, forging ahead in her economic development, beginning to overcome her domestic problems, her GNP nearing the trillion-dollar mark and nearly ten times that of any European power, could be the natural leader?

## II

The growing dependence of Western Europe on the United States in security, in industry and in technology leads to an increasing subordination of European policies to American interests. Revived concern about European security makes governments anxious to retain American protection. They shape their foreign policies so that they become compatible with American objectives, and are eager to avoid any friction with their mighty and, for the most part, trusted ally and protector.

Separately, security considerations and technological dependence may not provide a firm basis for Atlanticization. The desire for national independence is too potent to be permanently abdicated by a crisis; fear is subject to changing assessments of danger and may diminish again with an alteration in Soviet policy or Soviet leadership, or an American breakthrough in defence technology. Technological dependence, 'industrial helotry',[5] does not by itself imply political helotry. As Jean-Jacques Servan-Schreiber has written, 'The economic satellization of Europe would not prevent the French from discussing politics nor the Germans from going to concerts.'[6] The

[5] Harold Wilson's phrase before the Consultative Assembly of the Council of Europe, 23 January 1967, reported in *The Times*, 24 January 1967.
[6] Jean-Jacques Servan-Schreiber, *Le Défi américain* (Paris: Denoël, 1967), p. 210. Translation by Ronald Steel, *The American Challenge* (London: Hamish Hamilton; New York: Atheneum, 1968), p. 139.

amount of American vested interests in Western Europe may even provide an effective leverage for Europeans to increase their political standing *vis-à-vis* the American administration. As the United States acquires more vulnerable assets in Europe, she may be more amenable to considering European interests, and the less competitive European firms become, the more intense will be the struggle among American competitors to secure orders in European markets.

Yet Western Europe is hardly in a position to exert influence politically. Not even while the 'unification of Europe, that still untapped source of great potential strength' seemed to remain an open option, was the disparity of reactions to American investment in different West European countries overcome and a common response formulated.[7] Now that West Europeans have given up hope of political union and have accepted American predominance, this source of strength has been cut off. West European states can exert only individual influence through bilateral relationships in which American preponderance leaves them little scope for manœuvre.

The combination of security concerns and industrial dependence succeeds in restricting the political autonomy of West European governments. Although they are under no formal compulsion, their own interests demand that they give priority to American objectives. This is most obvious in defence: accepting the American strategic guarantee implies that the strategic interests of the United States may not be challenged by West European governments;[8] relying on sophisticated American weapons for their armed forces – aircraft and missiles, for instance – West Europeans have to endorse, for the most part, the military requirements laid down by American planners; as modern aircraft and electronics systems become more complex, West European governments lose even the

---

[7] Christopher Layton, *Trans-Atlantic Investments*, The Atlantic Papers (Paris: Atlantic Institute, 1968), pp. 30–48 and 141.

[8] Even in a stronger Europe, this would be a major problem, see Chapter five (*Partnership Europe*). For a Europe independent in its defence see Chapter six (*Independent Federal Europe*).

theoretical possibility of producing their own weapons without American help. West European defence policies become an element of American defence policy.

A similar process is under way in the field of foreign policy. Here, too, West Europeans come to realize the limits of independence. The instruments of commercial policy that form part of the arsenal of foreign policy are largely taken out of their hands. In their relations with the United States they relinquish trade and capital restrictions and accept American leadership in monetary matters. And in their relations with Eastern Europe and the Third World, West European governments, from caution rather than compulsion, must increasingly take American politico-industrial interests into account. Perhaps even more important, West European governments, because of their consideration for American interests, adopt a primarily conservative approach to foreign policy, avoiding political risks. No longer wishing to change the *status quo* in Europe, they are content to cultivate their gardens under American tutelage.

*Atlanticized Europe* does not require strong European institutions nor, for that matter, new Atlantic institutions. As the network of American influence spreads over Western Europe, governments act in a common pattern; as they accept American leadership, their relations with the United States can be based on an informal footing. This has the advantage of not exposing Western Europe's subservience to American leadership, and the particular advantage of being flexible enough not to be jeopardized by possible dissenters from Atlanticization – like France – which, despite American predominance, struggle to retain national independence.

The European Communities are maintained, but change in character as they adjust to the requirements of Atlanticization. They continue to organize economic policy in Western Europe, but American industrial interests are represented *de facto* in the Commission and the Council of Ministers, so that common European policies comply with the short-term interests of American pressure groups, for instance in energy, science, agriculture, monetary policy.[9] European economic integration is no longer intended to serve European economic independence, nor even to provide the framework for elaboration of a specifically European as opposed to an American viewpoint. An Atlantic economic structure, based on free trade and unrestricted access to the markets of member countries may seem the logical conclusion. It would incorporate the European Customs Union and provide a minimum of organizational machinery to supervise such things as government aid to exports, tax harmonization, credit arrangements in East-West trade, but without involving a pooling of sovereignty and the delegation of national powers to any form of Atlantic supra-national authority.[10]

NATO is strengthened and broadens its scope. Defence becomes only one, though still the most formalized, of its responsibilities. American strategic concepts and their fluctuations cease to be disputed by West European governments. Britain, and perhaps even France, assign their nuclear forces to NATO control, reduce their nuclear research programmes and accept in practice, though not perhaps formally, that there is only one effective centre of nuclear command and control in the Alliance. Defence co-operation is streamlined under American guidance; joint arms procurement becomes in practice largely procurement from the United States or of American designs; logistic chains are standardized on American standards; and specialized roles within the American concept for European defence are allocated to the nations of the Alliance.[11]

In addition machinery is set up for frequent and regular consultations on all matters of mutual concern among heads of government, foreign, defence and finance ministers. Under

[9] Club Jean Moulin, *Pour une Politique étrangère de l'Europe*, Paris, 1966, p. 24.

[10] See Maxwell Stamp Associates, 'The Free Trade Area Option', *The Atlantic Trade Study* (London, 1967), p. 27.

[11] See Edmund Stillman, Herman Kahn and Anthony J. Wiener, *Alternatives for European Defence in the Next Decade* (Croton-on-Hudson, N.Y.: Hudson Institute, 1964), p. 101.

the NATO Council, specialized bodies of permanent representatives are installed, whose task it is to co-ordinate West European and American policy, and to ensure consideration for those European objectives that are compatible with American interests. Co-ordination is made possible by the conviction of Europeans that their fate is irrevocably linked to that of the United States; her failure is their failure, her success their success.

## III

Does this provide a stable basis for Western Europe in the 1970s? Although it may be easier to achieve stability in an alliance if one partner is recognized as the undisputed leader, the strains and stresses are still considerable. They have bedevilled European–American relations throughout the 1960s when Atlanticization was still over the horizon, and even then have often enough seemed to widen the Atlantic Ocean rather than narrow it, to increase anti-Americanism in Europe and irritation with Europe in the United States. *Atlanticized Europe*, implying complete West European acceptance of American leadership, may be an entirely unworkable model.

The difficulties will not, in the first instance, emanate from reluctance to align European foreign and defence policies with those of the United States. West Europeans have, during the 1950s and most of the 1960s, become accustomed to doing this particularly in defence policy. Moreover, in foreign policy West European governments will find themselves in agreement with American views and actions more often than not, and it will be possible to achieve co-ordination without any great pressure from the United States. Since West Europeans regard the super-power relationship as something they can no longer significantly affect, the frictions in European–American relations that arose in the 1960s out of European distrust of the Washington–Moscow dialogue, will be less apparent in *Atlanticized Europe*. Similarly, the discord that resulted from an

American concept of the United States as a world policeman, will fade as the United States refines and limits that concept of her role. The end of the Vietnam War will mark a new era in this respect. President Nixon, who can hardly be suspected of entertaining 'dovish' attitudes, has made this quite clear when summing up the lesson of Vietnam for the United States: 'If another friendly country should be faced with an externally supported Communist insurrection – whether in Asia, or in Africa or even in Latin America – there is a serious question whether the American public or the American Congress would now support a unilateral American intervention, even at the request of the host government.'[12] This attitude is more to the linking of West Europeans, and American leadership will be more readily accepted if there is little risk of involvement in distant conflict as a result of American commitments outside Europe.

But it is not only the elimination of divergent trends of European and American interests that will make American leadership more palatable to West European states. There will be a general shift of political emphasis from foreign policy towards domestic matters in Europe, and not only in Europe. All industrialized societies will have to cope with the crisis of modernization, already manifest in the social unrest of the late 1960s. They will have to adapt their political and social structures, dating from the nineteenth or the early twentieth century, to the emerging patterns of the 'Technetronic Society', with all the problems this entails for democratic communications, for the control of political and economic power, education and the distribution of welfare.[13] West European societies, lacking the mobility, the dynamism and the acceptance of change that characterize their American counterpart, and imprisoned in old-fashioned conventions and rules, may find this a task that absorbs their political energy to the full. They may consequently be ready to hand over a large measure

[12] 'Asia after Vietnam', *Foreign Affairs*, October 1967, p. 114.
[13] See Z. Brzezinski, 'America in the Technetronic Age', *Encounter*, January 1968, p. 16.

of responsibility for dealing with the problems of international politics to the United States.

Abdication of an independent role in foreign and defence policy, and absorption with domestic problems do not, however, imply that European–American relations in *Atlanticized Europe* will be harmonious. The contrary will be the case: because the United States is deeply involved in the domestic affairs of Western Europe, relations between them encounter the bitterness and controversy of internal upheaval in Europe; emotions may run so high that dependence on the United States is discounted, and a new generation of European élites overruled in their trust and admiration for a new generation of American leaders. It would not be the dominance of the United States in foreign policy that would breed popular resentment in Western Europe, so much as the attempt to make European social and economic life conform to American standards, whatever material benefits might accrue to it.

American industrial activity in Europe and Europe's subsequent close association with technological progress in the United States, will make Western Europe flourish economically, a prosperous colony of American capital, know-how, and management. But while colonies may be prosperous, they are rarely satisfied and never grateful.[14] The further American economic invasion proceeds, the more European industry is streamlined by American business methods, the deeper European resentment will run. It will not, in the first place, be resentment against American ownership. American firms in Europe are gradually internationalizing their staff, and may even have reached a point 'where they and not even the most enlightened national governments are the true Evangelists of a genuinely international society and economy'.[15] It will be resentment against the brutality of progress, against the yardstick of efficiency and cost-effectiveness that the new industrial methods impose on European society.

[14] Club Jean Moulin, *Pour une Politique étrangère de l'Europe*, p. 28.
[15] Harry G. Johnson, 'The Phoney War', *Interplay*, Vol. 2, No. 1, June–July 1968, p. 59.

Although this development will not necessarily be linked with the American industrial presence in Europe, it will be regarded as a result of this presence. The suspicion and concern with which many Europeans view American investment in their countries reveals, as Jean-Jacques Servan-Schreiber has rightly point out, 'the fear of a future that was chosen by their fathers when they launched the first industrial revolution and which they themselves reaffirmed by starting the second'.[16] The industrialist who has lost control of his firm to the American partner, the shopkeeper whose business is suffocated by supermarkets, the employee who cannot adjust to changing management methods, in short, all those left behind in the speedy process of change will constitute a formidable reservoir of dissatisfaction and resentment for reactionary political movements that oppose social, educational and ethical changes under the banners of nationalism, neutralism and anti-Americanism. They will be joined by domestic Communist forces in Western Europe, representing a considerable proportion of voters in France and Italy, and by embittered Europeanists who blame the United States for the destruction of their hopes of a politically united Europe.[17]

These expressions of political anti-Americanism will be of different strength in different countries and may not be strong enough anywhere to affect the fundamental assumptions of *Atlanticized Europe*, that Europe's future is tied to the dominant American ally; but they will affect at least the atmosphere of European–American relations in almost every country. Anti-Americanism and neutralism will be fashionable with voters, especially the new generation, and all political parties, even those in favour of Atlanticization, will have to make concessions to them. The more American influence limits the scope of their independent action, the more anxious governments will be to prove their independence of it. They will continue to pretend that the final decisions are theirs, even if

[16] J.-J. Servan-Schreiber, *Le Défi américain*, p. 213; *The American Challenge*, p. 142.
[17] See Club Jean Moulin, *Pour une Politique étrangère de l'Europe*, p. 29.

the centre of decision-making has long been removed from Europe to the United States. This will create an ever-growing 'credibility-gap' between the words and the deeds of governments and, in time, stir up further domestic unrest.

The internal situation of *Atlanticized Europe* will be particularly awkward if any West European state should succeed in resisting the process of Atlanticization. France would be the most likely country, even after President de Gaulle's departure from the political scene, to attempt a continuing policy of independence from the United States. This would, of course, require a high degree of political will: France, like other West European countries, has felt the impact of the American industrial invasion and, in spite of her political views, has not been prepared, in the 1960s, to take effective counter-measures. She would have to improve upon her present efforts in the field of technology, but even then her industrial competitiveness would be inferior to that of the other, Atlanticized, European states. She would have to accept this position as the necessary price of independence, a difficult choice to make in a world where economic progress and political influence are closely intertwined. Yet France in the 1960s has, to a certain extent, defied this thesis, and *Atlanticized Europe* may offer even to a France that is industrially less advanced than her neighbours a margin of political manœuvre, not only in relation to Eastern Europe and the Soviet Union, but also in Western Europe, where France would serve as a symbol of independence and nationalism, and a centre of attraction for the forces of anti-Americanism. She might persuade other countries to follow her lead, and Germany, frustrated by the fear that *Atlanticized Europe* would perpetuate her national division, could be one of the first to do so, unless the danger of war in Europe, one of the justifications for *Atlanticized Europe*, remains great and constant. At any rate, an independent France would aggravate *Atlanticized Europe's* internal instability.

IV

For those who believe that 'what is good for General Motors is good for the United States', *Atlanticized Europe* would seem America's favourite choice. Uninhibited access to a large European market of two hundred million people with a high standard of living would, no doubt, be a source of gratification to the American industrialist and business man. But, contrary to Marxist belief, American foreign policy is not dictated by corporation presidents, and to the policy-makers and for public opinion in the United States the advantages would be less clear. In the first place, *Atlanticized Europe* would represent failure of American post-war policy. This policy has been to encourage West European integration and unity, hoping for a strong, dynamic and friendly European partner, not a resigned, impotent or servile group of militarily or technologically beholden clients. If in this conception it had been assumed that the United States would be the natural leader of a continuing European–American alliance, at least it was to be leadership by consent and not by submission.

In some respects the creation of a centralized Atlantic military and economic system under clear American leadership would offer certain advantages for American policy. The power of her NATO allies to impede or complicate American decisions would diminish, and the use of American power would no longer be checked by a necessity of obtaining European agreement. The dialogue with the Soviet Union, the only power of her own weight in international politics, would no longer be disturbed by European obstinacy or suspicion. Crises, political or economic, could be managed more efficiently by a concentration of decision-making in Washington than they are by the present mixture of traditional diplomacy and multilateral consultation in the NATO Council or the Group of Ten. In the past, Americans may have had reason to fear a 'political-military union of Europe which would lead to a political separation of Europe from America', but in *Atlanticized Europe* this fear would be removed, if not for ever, at least for the foreseeable future.[18]

Nevertheless, the United States would be drawn, however reluctantly, into greater responsibility for Western Europe. By assuming the role of co-ordinator of European policies, she would be bound to become involved in the political decision-making process of West European governments, even against her own intentions. If *Atlanticized Europe* came about as the result of increased tension in Europe or a deteriorating relationship with the Soviet Union, it would mean maintaining the same level of American military forces in Europe as in the 1960s, perhaps even raising the level; this would conflict with a widely held American view that the United States is over-committed in general, and in particular is bearing too large a proportion of the burden of collective defence in Europe. And if *Atlanticized Europe* were not the consequence of increased East-West tension but merely of a decline in Western Europe's ability to compete and co-operate, there would be equally little prospect of trimming the burden. American involvement in European decision-making would be most obvious in crises, economic or military, but would also shape day-to-day policy-making in European capitals.

It would be this extent of American political involvement in Western Europe, that would irritate both European and American public opinion. While the United States would be prepared to lead in an emergency, for instance, a revival of tension in Central Europe, as she has done in the past, she would respond less easily to the demands of exerting the dominant external influence in the politics of a number of highly vocal democracies. The traditional American discomfort in a position of dominance would be particularly acute in *Atlanticized Europe*. Senator Fulbright's warning of the late 1960s, could become the overwhelming American belief in the 1970s: 'Gradually but unmistakably America is showing signs of that arrogance of power which has affected, weakened, and

[18] Harold van B. Cleveland, *The Atlantic Idea and its European Rivals* (New York and London: McGraw-Hill, 1966), p. 162.

in some cases destroyed great nations in the past. In so doing we are not living up to our capacity and promise as a civilized example for the world.'[19] The desire to return to the 'traditional American values which hold that co-operation in consensus, not conflict, are the norm in international relations, and that power without consent is *ipso facto* evil' could only grow stronger in response to anti-Americanism and national restnessness in Europe.[0]

*Atlanticized Europe*, therefore, would not provide a stable basis for European–American relations in the next decade, and both West Europeans and Americans would realize it. However resigned to a subordinate role, West European governments would be little more than reluctant and passive allies of the United States. However prepared to heed European concerns and to lead the Alliance in a generous spirit, irritation with Europe and doubts about her own role in the relationship might make the United States an impatient and inconsiderate leader. Instead of cementing the American–European relationship, *Atlanticized Europe* would, in fact, erode it. Even though it might be the consequence of a deterioration in Soviet-American relations, it might be the model which would lead most rapidly to some sort of super-power bargain about Europe.

For Soviet policy, *Atlanticized Europe* represents the failure of several decades of endeavour since it strengthens and entrenches the American position in Western Europe. The fact that it also entrenches the *status quo* in Europe and once again divides the Continent into two distinct political systems would not counterbalance this failure. The reaction of the Soviet Union and the East European countries will differ however, according to the circumstances that bring *Atlanticized Europe* into being.

If Western Europe becomes increasingly dominated by the United States as a result of her technological prowess and her

[19] J. William Fulbright, *The Arrogance of Power* (New York: Random House), p. 22.
[20] Harold van B. Cleveland, *op. cit.*, p. 166.

increased control of European industry, the Soviet reaction will be to pursue a political strategy aimed at encouraging the restlessness of individual West European countries. One Soviet argument will be that 'in the sphere of international trade Western Europe and the United States are competitors and rivals, and their interests in this sphere tend to clash more sharply than those, say, of Western and Eastern Europe, where, moreover, broad possibilities for business co-operation on a mutually advantageous basis have appeared in the last few years'.[21] Russia might realize that the United States was superior in every respect to any combination of even ten West European countries, but would argue that this superiority should be an additional impetus for the Europeans to strive for independence, and offer her co-operation to meet the need for technological partners.

Any West European politician or businessman can see the flaws in this argument. But it contains the basis of a psychological argument which might successfully blur the economic and scientific realities of the situation, and in which the Soviet Union can expect some East European support. The 'American challenge' by this argument, is not so much proof of American efficiency as of the willingness of certain Europeans to betray the independence and traditions of their continent. Speaking for Eastern Europe, a Polish reviewer of J.-J. Servan-Schreiber's book stated in 1968: 'We similarly feel ourselves to be the inheritors of European culture and civilization and its greatest humanistic values: for this we share his concern over its threatened Americanization.'[22]

It is a somewhat risky argument for the Soviet Union to use, partly because it might increase the feeling in Eastern Europe (which is interested in getting technological know-how from any source) that 'Europeanism' implies freedom from domination by both super-powers; partly because of her uncertainty

[21] V. Osipov, 'New Trends on the Continent', *International Affairs* (Moscow), July 1967, p. 15.

[22] W. Leder, *Nowe Drogi*, March 1968; reprinted in *Polish Perspectives*, June 1968.

as to whether she really does want the United States out of Europe altogether. But it might serve as a divisive technique in Western Europe, for instance, to concentrate on reminding France and Italy of their European affiliations, while pointing to the servility of Germany and Britain.

If *Atlanticized Europe* came into being as the result of a prolonged crisis or a deterioration of security in Europe, the Soviet Union would consider herself highly vulnerable *vis-à-vis* this American empire extending from the Elbe to the Pacific. She would strive to tighten and extend her control in Eastern Europe and the Mediterranean. She would have to give no further thought to the modification of her basic policy on German reunification or other outstanding European issues; the positions of the Cold War would simply be reaffirmed.

But whatever the initial cause of *Atlanticized Europe*, the Soviet Union would regard it as a failure of her post-war policy; the United States would be more deeply committed and present in Europe than ever and all Soviet efforts to persuade the West European powers that they can co-exist with the East without the presence of American troops, and can dispense with NATO, would have proved fruitless. Her failure would not be lost on her East European allies.

If the countries of Western Europe have ceased to be independent and interesting interlocutors for the Soviet Union, if Eastern Europe is basically restless, even though temporarily under firmer Soviet control, is not the logical step for the Soviet Union to negotiate a European settlement with the United States and impose it while both still possess the power to do so?

## V

There is no country in Western Europe for whom *Atlanticized Europe* would be advantageous – nor does it possess any real attraction for the United States. All the European countries would find their freedom of manœuvre reduced, including countries such as France that might somehow succeed in staying outside the sphere of immediate American dominance. It is perhaps less galling a prospect for the smaller countries, who have always preferred American leadership to that of any of the European middle powers, but even they would not be immune to the traditional temptation of a neutralist or even neutral alternative. Britain which encouraged the United States to take a leading role in European affairs in the post-war years, would have to give up any ambition to play an active part in the West European structure and resign herself to the status of a client nation. For Germany, this model offers no hopes for the solution of her national problem nor of improving her relations with Eastern Europe.

*Atlanticized Europe* is a situation that, unlike the other models, could develop by inadvertence, almost by accident, at any rate by failure to evolve a practicable alternative. But because it came about inadvertently it would not necessarily be transitory.

The very undesirability of *Atlanticized Europe* may provide the incentive for the United States and Western Europe to put their relationship on a new basis. But if Western Europe should drift into Atlanticization, the chance for a more harmonious structure of European–American relations would be lost for a long time. Anti-Americanism in Europe and irritation with Europe in America would exclude any form of partnership; the European desire to throw off the American yoke would leave but two possible directions for policy-makers: either European independence or nationalist fragmentation.

Chapter Three

# EUROPE DES ETATS

## I

Unlike *Evolutionary* and *Atlanticized Europe*, this is a Europe whose member states aspire to a distinctive role in world politics and are confident of their importance and power; unlike those of *Fragmented Europe*[1] they share a common political attitude, but this community of view is not channelled into strong institutions and political structures as it is in *Independent Europe*;[2] the nation state remains the focus of action and decision.

*Europe des Etats* is not, strictly speaking, a Gaullist Europe, simply because there does not seem to be a truly European Gaullist philosophy. As Edmond Jouve characterized the European policy of President de Gaulle: 'The construction of Europe is only desirable, and only to be pursued to the extent that it lifts France to the first rank.'[3] For de Gaulle, Europe is a means of raising the status of France, rather than the participation of France being a means of improving the position of Europe. Nevertheless, many of the ideas expressed by President de Gaulle can be applied to Europe as a whole; developed for the grandeur of France, they may serve the grandeur of Europe. The aim is no longer a political structure limited to Western Europe, but one encompassing the whole of Europe. Europe's weakness resides in its artificial division into an Eastern and a Western part. As long as Europe is divided, it must be subordinated to the two great powers, the United States and the Soviet Union. But Europe must overcome this

[1] See Chapter Four.
[2] See Chapter Six.
[3] Edmond Jouve, *Le Général de Gaulle et la construction de l'Europe (1940–1966)*, Tome I (Paris: Librairie Général de Droit, 1967), p. 722.

division in order to escape from the subordination. The unity of Europe must be restored in order to regain the 'historical existence which is more natural and, in the long run, more real than any ideological or strategic cleavage',[4] enable Europe to exercise the responsibility that derives from its cultural and historical heritage, and to help safeguard world peace. Strengthened by unity and independence, the European states can achieve the last by using their weight to create a state of equilibrium between the super-powers and by setting an example in the Third World.

West European leaders realize that the unification of Europe is still a long way off. But they feel that they must take the first step, organizing their part of Europe so that it may serve as the cornerstone of an eventual pan-European edifice. West European countries must, therefore, loosen their ties with the United States and pursue independent policies. To provide the nucleus of a union '*de l'Europe tout entière*', they must co-operate in a way that does not impede the ultimate adhesion of the East European states to a European political and economic system. Western Europe must co-ordinate its objectives rather than build a political structure of its own. The unity of Europe, since it exists already in its cultural and philosophical aspects, does not require a formal structure for co-operation and common decision-making, at least for the time being or in its Western half alone; what is more important is a general consensus of political views among West European states.

## II

*Europe des Etats* is the product of a deliberate decision to place diminishing emphasis on existing European organizations. The European Communities in Brussels are gradually divested of their supra-national element. The Commission becomes a

[4] Pierre Hassner: 'Polycentrism, West and East: Implications of the Western Debates', in Kurt London, *Eastern Europe in Transition* (Baltimore: Johns Hopkins Press, 1966).

secretariat with administrative functions only, and is firmly subordinated to the Council of Ministers, which becomes the only source of political power in the communities. Economic co-operation is no longer regarded as the first requisite of political union, but simply as one technique which will enable Western Europe to pursue its political aims, complementary to the political autonomy of the nation state, and in no way intended to replace it. Britain and the Scandinavian countries become members of this attenuated Community, but, though they accept the general view of their neighbours that the restoration of European unity and independence is the prime objective, EEC is no longer an important factor in their policy.

The Atlantic Alliance survives as a collective security arrangement like SEATO, but the integrated military machinery and the command structure of NATO are gradually dismantled. Defence becomes once again a primarily national concern. There is no integrated European defence organization. France and Britain retain their nuclear forces which are explicitly designed to serve as a minimum deterrent force for Western Europe;[5] but there is no co-ordination with American strategic planning, and Anglo-American arrangements in the nuclear field have been ended. The other West European states accept this situation and with it a privileged position for the nuclear powers in defence matters. Germany, now responsible for her own defence, remains faithful to her obligation under the Non-Proliferation Treaty not to build a national nuclear force, and accepts the necessary inspection system, but she rebuilds a general staff and the full apparatus of national military planning. There is no joint arms procurement among the West European members of the Alliance but a general policy of 'Buy European First'. The co-ordination of policies between West European states is implemented in a series of frequent and regular consultations on all subjects of common interest, which take place behind the scenes at the

[5] G. Pompidou: 'L'existence d'une puissance atomique francaise sera pour cette Europe en gestation une garantie nouvelle,' in E. Jouve, *De Gaulle*, Tome I, pp. 641–2.

EEC or WEU Councils, at the level of ministers and senior civil servants and, occasionally, heads of government. There is no majority vote in either Council; decisions are taken unanimously, states are only bound to those decisions they have agreed to. In short, Western Europe forms a union of states along the lines of the second Fouchet Plan in order to draw together, co-ordinate and unify the policies of the member states in areas of common interest: foreign policy, economy, culture and defence.[6]

Their main interest lies in 'European reconciliation', and their political energy is chiefly directed towards establishing closer ties with the countries of Eastern Europe. They are eager to avoid all measures that would endanger this development. Treaties of non-aggression between East and West European states are proposed to settle the issue of security and to open the way to more liberal trade arrangements and cultural exchanges.

The structure of *Europe des Etats*, therefore, is a function of *détente*. The model is only conceivable in the absence of any general military threats, and therefore in the absence of endemic political crises in East–West relations: Western Europe deliberately chooses military and organizational weakness in order to gain political strength. The analysis of the advantages and disadvantages of the model must take this into account; they must be judged in the context of *détente* alone, and *détente* must be the background for examining whether it is workable or capable of living up to its pretensions.

## III

What political circumstances in the 1970s might bring about the external conditions and the political consensus within Western Europe that would make this model feasible? What once seemed the eccentric idea of an elderly general has already, in the 1960s, gained some ground and infiltrated the

[6] Article II, reprinted in E. Jouve, *De Gaulle*, Tome II, pp. 445–9.

thinking of various political groups from the right wing of the CDU in Germany to Conservative leaders in Britain and to left-wing movements in Italy.[7] There is no *a priori* reason why it should not make further headway in the next decade. If security loses its priority as a result of prolonged *détente*, even for the more security-minded countries, none of them will see the necessity to make special efforts to satisfy their American ally, and what were doubts about the American readiness to risk a nuclear war for the defence of Europe in the 1960s, may become a firm conviction. The American technological invasion of Europe, formerly welcomed by at least some West European governments, may extend to a point where it provokes universal resentment and resistance in Western Europe. The uneasiness about the role of the dollar in the international monetary system may lead to united opposition to American views.

A basis of agreement also seems conceivable in West European attitudes towards the Soviet Union. Undisturbed *détente* aided by conservative Soviet leadership will have done away with the cold-war image of Soviet aggressiveness, even in the eyes of the more vigilant governments. Moreover, in their concern to overcome the division of Europe, West European governments will come to see Russia as European and a more natural partner in their dialogue than the distant world power of the United States; they may feel they can do so at reduced risk having sensed that the United States has finally outdistanced the Soviet Union in the super-power race.[8]

It may be even easier to get agreement on the structure of West European co-operation. In every country civil servants, and many politicians too, distrust international organizations and believe firmly in the nation state; a loose structure of European co-operation which leaves the states' sovereignty intact, is easy to agree on since it asks for little or no sacrifice of national autonomy.

[7] See O. Pick and R. Tilford, 'Gaullism Beyond the Rhine', *International Journal*, 1968, p. 234.

[8] This possibility is sketched in George Liska, *Imperial America* (Baltimore: Johns Hopkins Press, 1967), pp. 65f.

However, agreement among West European states on general conceptions and hypotheses will be insufficient to form a firm coalition of power. It offers no specific guidelines for day-to-day policies, leaving each member state to cope with its problems alone. There is no framework of continuous co-operation among West Europeans who, though indulging in declarations of solidarity, may wonder how much they can really count on each other's support. Even if European solidarity should survive the revival of nationalism, Italy, the Scandinavian countries and Benelux will distrust the larger powers of France, Germany and Britain, and these three middle powers might distrust each other or a combination of the other two. The rule of unanimity in decision-making, which theoretically leaves every government to decide whether or not it will be bound by a common decision, will increase such apprehension; the smaller countries will find themselves forced to conform with the bigger ones if they are not to be excluded from joint ventures altogether, just as the larger ones will want to exert pressure on them in order to rally them to their views.

Rivalry, envy and nationalism may emerge and replace the West European reconciliation of the post-war years. Inter-European relations in *Europe des Etats* will be competitive rather than co-operative. Co-operation will be limited to those fields least affecting national sovereignty and, consequently, joint policy-making will be restricted to the lowest common denominator of agreement between the major states. In the absence of a long-term structural commitment that might break the vicious circle of *juste retour*, each of the West European states will be eager to build a firm national base of science and technology before embarking on joint projects, which will be bedevilled by the inefficiency, procrastination and frustration that accompanied inter-governmental negotiations on so many joint ventures of the 1960s. In defence, after the dissolution of NATO, planning will again be a national matter, and national military planners, while postulating a co-ordination of European views, will, in fact, be prepared to accept co-ordination only if their own views prevail. A common policy to cope with the problems related to the inflow of American capital into Europe will be jeopardized by lists of exceptions submitted by governments to safeguard their differing national interests: Belgium and Italy might favour a liberal policy, France and Germany might prefer a more protectionist one. In foreign aid, each West European government will have its favourites in the developing world, and be unwilling to sacrifice them for a common European policy. The European Communities, shorn of a Commission which has the power of initiative, will cease to provide a framework within which diverging economic policies can be moulded into some common form; the Treaties of Paris and Rome, which though specific on the abolition of discrimination within the Common Market, generalize on the contents of common policies, will lose their unifying momentum.

*Europe des Etats* will be a Europe of words rather than of action. It may succeed in increasing cultural exchanges among European states and in printing European stamps, but it will fail to augment European independence. Instead of creating an equilibrium between the super-powers, Europe will, industrially and strategically, remain under their influence.

It would, however, seem a more realistic choice if one of its members were strong enough to serve as a unifying force, to impose its views on the others and unite them behind it. The Gaullist claim of French leadership in this Europe, far from being incompatible with the European idea, may be the very condition for making *Europe des Etats* work. Only under firm and convincing leadership can the centrifugal powers of a concert of nation states be channelled into a common position, and the inherent dangers of instability and secession be avoided.

But French leadership is unlikely to be convincing, either to the member states of Europe or to the super-powers. France in the 1970s may be less in a position to lead Europe than in the 1960s, other than by vetoing common efforts. Her economic limitations will have put a brake on her political ambitions.

Her strategic power, already somewhat impeded by economic and technological obstacles, may be insufficient to justify a claim to leadership. It consumes a high proportion of her scientific and economic potential and may hamper her progress in civil technology and make it hard for her to match the industrial achievements of Germany, Italy and Britain. Moreover, no West European country has a bigger job of internal modernization than France. The imposing personality of President de Gaulle, his skill and his charisma, may have succeeded, in the 1960s, in making France's neighbours take ambitions for power. After de Gaulle's departure, however, the two will be separated and France may again be measured by the yardstick of power alone. She will remain an important country but not one whose position commands a special allegiance from her neighbours. This would be particularly obvious if Britain was no longer left outside the European concert.

Nor could Britain provide the strong leadership that would be necessary to make *Europe des Etats* work. Her strategic power is also limited, more limited than France's if she abandons her agreements with the United States. Her technological capacity, though greater than that of France, is not adequate to make her an alternative source of dynamism to the United States. Moreover, there is a certain legacy of scepticism about her credentials as a Western European power which it may take a considerable time to overcome, even assuming that her political life produces powerful leaders in the 1970s.

Nor would a Franco-British condominium, based on their nuclear forces, provide the required leadership for *Europe des Etats*. Even if their combined strategic and technological power should theoretically justify such a claim to leadership, they would have to enter into a much closer relationship with each other in order to apply this power. This would necessitate an effective merging of their national identities, of the kind that Churchill proposed in the desperate spring of 1940, a structure of bilateral supra-nationalism, which would run counter to every principle of *Europe des Etats*.

One of the remaining possibilities is leadership by a Franco-German condominium, which, since there is no question of having to pool nuclear weapons, could take the form of an *entente*, a working partnership rather than a merging of sovereignty. In some senses such an *entente* already exists and has since the signing of the Franco-German Treaty in 1963. But if it were used as the basis of a claim to leadership in a *Europe des Etats* there is the question of how acceptable it would be to Britain or to the smaller countries. There is an even bigger question whether the exercise of leadership by reliance on German agreement and support would be acceptable to France, given the fact that she would be the weaker partner in terms of economic power, and that acting in double harness with Germany would create special problems for France in her relations with Eastern Europe and the Soviet Union, thus negating one of the objectives of a *Europe des Etats*.

## IV

Without a common structure to mould diverging West European policies into a common form, without a leader who might compensate for the lack of organization, *Europe des Etats* does not provide a stable framework for West European co-operation. However, this does not necessarily mean that it would not be a sensible choice for West European governments to take. If, in spite of its inherent contradictions and shortcomings, it promises success, in overcoming the division of Europe, *Europe des Etats*, might still provide an acceptable future. But does it promise success?

In theory, the countries of Eastern Europe would be delighted with *Europe des Etats*; it would facilitate those bilateral economic relations with a group of competitive Western Europe countries, which, as has already been suggested, suit their interests best and are still likely to in the 1970s. *Europe des Etats* would generally increase the freedom of manœuvre of East European states. While there is no direct connection between economic and political relations, *Europe des Etats* would weaken any Soviet argument for strengthening or further centralizing the machinery of COMECON for political purposes: moreover, if the West Europeans have demoted European security on their national agendas by allowing NATO to disintegrate, perhaps there is a prospect of a similar development within the Warsaw Pact, which was after all supposed to have been founded in response to the build-up of NATO. In general, *Europe des Etats*, with its emphasis on the nation state, appears to carry some prospects of greater independence for the East European countries, which are for the most part fiercely nationalist, but without necessarily alarming the ruling groups there by the prospect of their having to democratize their regimes or cease to be Communist. But nationalism is a double-edged weapon in Eastern Europe, and there are several countries which would have reason to fear the return of territorial disputes (over Macedonia and Transylvania for instance) which would result from a new Balkanization of Europe. The greatest difficulty for the East European states would be in accepting a fully independent Germany whose relations with East Germany and some other countries have not been finally settled, but which now has the full apparatus of national military power except nuclear weapons. The prospect becomes even less appealing in Eastern Europe if, in the interests of minimal cohesion in Western Europe, some diarchic leadership of Germany plus a nuclear power, either France or Britain, becomes imperative. In consequence, the more exposed East European countries might cling, to some form of Soviet guarantee, either bilateral or in the Warsaw Pact, which would partially negate the opportunity for greater independence that *Europe des Etats* is designed to offer them.

But most important for the East European reaction to *Europe des Etats* would be the attitude of the Soviet Union. She would be gratified to see the structure of co-operation in Western Europe disintegrating after the withdrawal of the United States and the end of NATO, and encouraged by the possibility which this new situation offered of negotiating a tacit or explicit arrangement with certain West European countries for the containment and isolation of Germany.

But at the same time, the Soviet Union would be aware of the deliberate challenge of *Europe des Etats* to her control over Eastern Europe, a challenge she has shown she takes very seriously by her interference in Czechoslovakia in August 1968. Besides *Europe des Etats* has gained momentum in Western Europe as an expression of a common European culture or consciousness which does not necessarily include the Soviet Union. And its appeal is partly that this 'Europe' is to become a counter-balancing force (though not necessarily in the strategic sense) between the two super-powers.[9] This is wholly unacceptable to the Soviet Union, first because she regards herself as European in a sense that the United States is not, and second, because she cannot accept a political divorce between herself and the countries of Eastern Europe. This attitude is no longer founded on strategic reasons alone, for Soviet planners have no reason to fear the onslaught of a handful of German divisions, though they have reason to fear the repercussions of European crises of all kinds which would arise more easily in a Europe in which super-power control had been removed. It is more because the adherence of the East European countries is essential both to her as the originator of the Communist State and as a symbol of her standing as a great power. Moreover, *Europe des Etats* would conflict with one deep-rooted, though not always predominant, strand of Soviet thought, namely that the *status quo* can only be maintained in Europe and its long-term security assured, if the United States plays an active part in European politics.

She would nominally welcome *Europe des Etats* but in reality have considerable reservations about it. She would try to prevent contacts between Eastern and Western Europe from becoming a source of political infection in the East, and she would attempt to ensure that the erosion of NATO did not

[9] For an examination of the complex power relations to which *Europe des Etats* might give rise, see Pierre Hassner, *Change and Security in Europe*, Part II, Adelphi Paper 49 (London: ISS, 1968), pp. 29–31.

eliminate her security relationship, bilateral or multilateral, with Eastern Europe. This model would be acceptable to the Soviet Union to the extent that it would weaken but not abolish the position of the United States in Europe and would loosen the Western alliance structure but not the Eastern. On the other hand, the emergence of nationalism, apart from its special significance in Germany, would cause Soviet concern because it would be part of a revival of nationalism throughout Europe, which might contribute to the disintegration of the Eastern bloc. *Europe des Etats* would be welcomed by at least some of the East European countries to the small extent that it weakened the position of the Soviet Union, but it would meet with reservations from them as far as it offered no genuine prospect for a future European settlement but simply encouraged German nationalism. None of the East European governments would be prepared to risk Soviet displeasure or even occupation by openly favouring *Europe des Etats*.

For the United States, *Europe des Etats* would imply a major change in her post-war policy towards Western Europe, and indeed her position in the world. This would not have to be a rapid shift; the American views about Europe have been of considerable continuity in the last twenty years and they would not change from one day to the next. American governments would continue, for some time, to support multilateralism in Europe and, perhaps, even hope that a co-ordination of West European policies within the framework of *Europe des Etats* would serve this aim as a step towards political union in Europe. The American school of thought that attaches greater priority to normalization of East–West relations than to the Atlantic concept, would welcome Western Europe's preoccupation with its relations with Eastern Europe.

But as *Europe des Etats* evolved, the need for the United States to change her policy would be pressing. The turning point would come when her European allies or the most important of them, told her that they would like the Atlantic Alliance to continue as a form of American guarantee and as a collective security system but that they wished to see an end of NATO and those forms of military integration in Western Europe, which in effect give the United States a high degree of control over the handling of a European crisis. At this point she would reply, most particularly in the American political climate of the 1970s when foreign commitments will be under the closest scrutiny, that she could give no form of specific guarantee to any group of West European countries unless they were prepared to maintain a multilateral politico-military system in which she had the last word. If they regarded this as incompatible with their desire for independence or as frustrating their relations with Eastern Europe, she would have two alternatives, either to withdraw from the Atlantic Alliance, leaving it to some other Western nuclear power to provide the necessary element of deterrence in Europe, and to reorganize her position in the world on a new multilateral alliance with Canada, Australia, the larger Latin American countries, and a Japan that was steadily growing more powerful; or to negotiate bilateral alliances with, say, Germany and Britain which would thereby, to a certain extent, opt out of the new European concert.

As the instability of *Europe des Etats* became clear, the United States would have little choice other than to concentrate on a close working partnership with the Soviet Union, if she wished to maintain a minimum of balance in Europe. Soviet-American co-operation, far from being disrupted by *Europe des Etats*, would be reinforced. In a certain sense, *Europe des Etats* would contribute to an equilibrium between the superpowers, not by its strength but by its weakness.

This Europe would, in the words of George Ball, result in 'weakening Atlantic relationships without a commensurate strengthening of European unity, and thus contribute to fragmentation rather than the building of a modern political structure'.[10] It would encourage rather than reconcile political divergences among West Europeans and thereby destroy, for

[10] George Ball, *The Discipline of Power* (London: Bodley Head; Boston: Atlantic-Little, Brown, 1968), p. 147.

a long time, the hope of building a politically coherent Europe. Even if it were successful in reducing Soviet control over Eastern Europe and bringing greater freedom of manœuvre to Poles, Czechs, Hungarians – and this is by no means certain – this success would be attributed to individual governments rather than to their collective efforts, thus further reducing the impetus towards European unity. However, this faint hope might induce governments to take the risks of *Europe des Etats*. But it seems a high risk. To Germany it offers, at the price of being reduced to a secondary role in Europe, no real hope for a settlement of her national problem, while increasing the danger of isolation. For France it holds a prospect not of acquiring great power status as a co-guarantor of European stability, but of being discredited as a medium power whose resources fall short of its ambitions. For Italy, Britain and Benelux it implies jeopardization of the Atlantic link without offering political compensation.

*Europe des Etats*, for these reasons, can only be a transitory Europe. West European policies, though identical in some matters, are different in others, and, in the absence of a structure to facilitate the hard business of continuous co-operation, the differences will make themselves felt. Furthermore, it is a conditional Europe, conceivable only in *détente*. If *détente*, already undermined by the Soviet invasion of Czechoslovakia in August 1968, should disappear, West European states will have nothing to fall back on.

The basic assumption of the model is, therefore, one of its basic weaknesses, as it evades the problem of security in Europe. It relies on an assumption based entirely on hypotheses about intentions and with no reference to capabilities. It is a pre-nuclear, almost a pre-twentieth-century model which overlooks, for instance, the fact that the Soviet Union could virtually obliterate any other European state overnight, or that, even in terms of conventional weapons, the level of armaments in Europe and their firepower has never been higher in time of peace and is higher than in any other area of the world. In its quite valid motive of East–West rapprochement and of minimizing the dominance of the super-powers, it neglects the fact that Europe is strewn with potential feuds and irredenta, or the way in which an unforeseen crisis can embroil countries against their better judgement, as happened in August 1914 or even in August 1968. It overlooks the fact that the Western powers in dismantling NATO and encouraging their East European friends to abolish the Warsaw Pact, would be dismantling complex forms of peace-keeping machinery without putting anything in their place.

If the model is to be taken seriously it cannot be studied in isolation from measures of European arms control so radical as to amount to a new European security system, in which the super-powers would be as much involved as the Europeans. One form of *Europe des Etats* that has attracted some support involves the creation of a Locarno type of agreement for some or all of the countries of Central, Eastern and Western Europe, in which they would have no alliance ties but would accept limitations on their forces and inspection of them, would agree to respect each other's territorial integrity and would be guaranteed against attack by each other and by the two super-powers, the system being managed by a European Security Organization. Another model would retain the two alliance systems, but without military integration, as methods of consultation between the guaranteed powers in Europe and their respective super-powers, while building a bridge between them by a European Security Council or Organization composed of representatives of both alliance systems. And there are other variations on the same theme.[11]

The essential point is that it by no means lies in the power of Western Europe alone to bring such ideas to fruition. Until there is the glimmering of a consensus between the two super-powers and the allies of each of them as to how European security can be organized more reasonably than by a confrontation of two military alliance systems whose internal

[11] For a brief examination of these models see Alastair Buchan, 'The Future of NATO', *International Conciliation*, October 1967. For a more detailed examination see Pierre Hassner, *Change and Security in Europe*, Part II.

effectiveness is largely dependent on their hostile image of the other, the pursuit of *Europe des Etats* holds more dangers than promises.

Chapter Four

# FRAGMENTED EUROPE

I

Most analyses of the futures of Western Europe, of its place in the world or its relationship to the super-powers, assume that it will continue to cohere economically and begin to cohere politically in the 1970s, or at least be inspired by a common motive. But why should this be so? If there is no pressing threat to the security of the West European states, if the strategic relationship between the United States and the Soviet Union remains a stable 'balance of prudence' – as a result of either technological developments or tacit agreement – if the penalties of co-ordinating national policies in bodies such as EEC or NATO appear to outweigh the advantages, then governments will begin to think increasingly in national terms. In a decade when social problems, in their widest sense, are likely to be complex and difficult to solve, the stability of governments will depend on their giving increased priority to national interests. Since these interests, if strictly interpreted, are by no means identical, and require different solutions, their policies towards each other, towards the East and towards the United States, will diverge.

*Fragmented Europe* shares certain features with *Europe des Etats*, notably a declining confidence in the value of institutional co-operation between governments. But it is a model in which 'the European idea' has receded completely, in which Frenchmen feel more Latin, Englishmen more Anglo-Saxon, Germans more Teuton, Scandinavians more Nordic than they feel European. In this model almost every government is wrestling with the problem of domestic discontent, ethnic minorities, urban unrest, or an alienated younger generation, for whom only national solutions seems to have significance. It

72

is a Western Europe of disillusioned states which have come to recognize that even by pooling their resources they can have no decisive influence on the overall pattern of international relations, so powerful are the forces of technological growth in the United States, the Soviet Union and Japan, so deep-rooted the sources of political unrest in the developing world. It is a Western Europe in which governments have come to believe that their salvation lies in abandoning any pretension to act in unison, and in co-operating instead with their immediate neighbours or else their traditional friends. The world is wide, the conception of the international system as a series of great regional blocs, which dominated the thinking of the 1950s and 1960s, is disappearing, and European conceptions change accordingly.[1] In face of a growing reluctance on the part of the United States to maintain her former degree of political and military commitment in Europe, West European governments are concerned that the two super-powers will gradually extend the scope of their understanding in strategic questions. They judge that neither super-power is prepared to be influenced by smaller powers in its dealings with the other, while both respect the other's fear of influence. West European states no longer see any virtue in placing primary emphasis on European or Atlantic arrangements. Instead, many of them prefer to make the United Nations and its specialized and regional organizations the focus of their international policy.

*Fragmented Europe* is by definition shorn of a common West European political structure. Any pretence that the Treaty of Rome is the basis of a European political system has naturally had to be abandoned. EEC remains as a customs union, but the European Commission has been disbanded. However, not all the existing institutions and bilateral arrangements in

[1] Some models of a fragmenting Europe assume an increasing number of European nuclear powers, e.g. Lincoln P. Bloomfield, *Western Europe to the Mid-Seventies Five Scenarios* (Cambridge, Mass.: Center for International Studies, M.I.T., 1968) or Edmund Stillman, Herman Kahn and Anthony J. Wiener, *Alternatives for European Defense in the Next Decade* (Croton-on-Hudson, N.Y.: Hudson Institute, 1964). This is not our assumption (see Chapter One) nor is it a necessary condition of a *Fragmented Europe*.

73

Europe need disappear. The Franco-German Treaty remains, though co-operation on defence becomes a dead letter. Western European Union remains for certain forms of European consultation, the Council of Ministers of EEC for others, the Atlantic Council for still others. All the non-nuclear powers in Western Europe are bound by the provisions of the Non-Proliferation Treaty whose inspection system has replaced that of Euratom. Nordic economic co-operation has been formalized.

The replacement of common interests by different policies becomes clear in the field which started post-war co-operation in Western Europe, that of defence. In France, President de Gaulle's successors remain committed to the *stratégie tous azimutus*, grounding France's security entirely on her own resources: the French nuclear submarine programme is expanded to twelve vessels and an ICBM is under development. But the internal dissensions of Western Europe have destroyed any illusion that this force could guarantee the security of other European countries, or somehow be held 'in trust' for a future European Union. French security policy is intended to create the basis of armed neutrality rather than French leadership of Western Europe: at the same time French diplomacy exploits France's traditional cultural links and friendship with certain countries in Eastern Europe, Poland and Rumania in particular, and also develops new links with the leading countries of the non-aligned world, India, Egypt and South Africa. France exercises her legal option and withdraws from the Atlantic Alliance after giving one year's notice. Belgium, with her African interests, becomes increasingly responsive to French policy. And there are strong voices in Italy arguing that, with her growing economic and political interests in Eastern Europe and the developing world, she should follow suit: these are counter-balanced for the time being by the fact that, with an active Soviet naval deployment in the Mediterranean, Italy faces a security problem which argues in favour of continued defence arrangements with the United States. Turkey adopts a policy resembling that of Iran, seeking equal relations with both super-powers. Greece regresses into a semi-permanent military regime which the United States and Western Europe shun.

Britain, for whom membership in the EEC has lost any political attractions, decides to construct an Atlantic Free Trade Area with the United States, Canada and other Commonwealth countries, and Japan, a decision that is made easier for Britain by the revival of the traditional Anglo-Japanese relationship and the development of complementary forms of advanced industry in the two island powers. But despite the fact that she has abandoned hope of entering a European economic arrangement, she now only possesses the military capability to operate in Europe. After investigation of alternatives such as an Anglo-French nuclear arrangement, she realizes that she can only remain a nuclear power at a cost that is reconcilable with economic growth and a high level of social services if she maintains a close nuclear partnership with the United States; the United States, anxious to retain an *interlocuteur valable* in a fragmenting Europe, is amenable to continuing such an arrangement: most of the old illusions about the 'special relationship' have, meanwhile, disappeared, leaving a Britain with a much less ambitious foreign policy than in the post-war decades. She is not, however, prepared to see the framework of collective security in Europe collapse.

The country that is placed in the most acute dilemma by this process of fragmentation in Europe is Germany. While other European countries may discover some compensation for the end of the European idea in strengthening their relations elsewhere – 'plurality of interests' becomes the fashionable phrase to describe this in European journalism and political speeches – Germany has no compensations. She remains the most exposed country in Western Europe with a continuing security problem. If the erosion of the Atlantic Alliance should continue to the point of its total collapse, she will have to take her security into her own hands. But, having signed the NPT, she has now lost the option of developing her own nuclear weapons to provide the basis of a national deterrent strategy comparable to that of France and Britain. And if she tries to rebuild the *Bundeswehr* on a purely national basis she risks damaging her relationship with Eastern Europe.

There are still divided views in Germany as to where her true interests lie; in adhering to the objective of reunification, which suggests a strong military position and the backing of as many allies as she can still muster; or in accepting East Germany as the second German state and trying to evolve the most workable relationship in trade, in technology, in free access, that is possible between a democratic and a Communist state, which suggests the unwisdom of a crash programme of national rearmament. There are also divided views as to who the most effective ally is likely to be; France, with her East European contacts, though French attention is now concentrated increasingly on relations with the developing world; Britain, who is still prepared to maintain some sort of multilateral defence system in Europe but is not greatly interested in the building of new structures in Western Europe; or the United States which alone possesses the strategic power to restrain Soviet pressure on Germany, and to help negotiate a new formula for the relationship between the two Germanies.

Germany's Western neighbours are subject to similar dilemmas, particularly the Netherlands and Denmark, who also feel that their security would be threatened by the collapse of the collective defence system, and who also fear acutely the revival of nationalism in Germany. Norway, her rising generation alienated from the United States by the violence of its society and fearful of being connected with a disintegrating Western Europe, revives her historic connection with Sweden and decides to withdraw from NATO, though not the Alliance.

But the United States is reluctant to undertake any major initiative or new commitment until her internal debate, the situation in the Far East and her relations with the Soviet Union have clarified. She has become increasingly disenchanted by her European commitments. Though the Vietnam conflict is over and American troops are no longer required there, a settlement has been achieved only at the price of considerable American humiliation which has deepened public disillusionment with foreign commitments. The administrations of the 1970s are under strong pressure to invest greater public resources in the regeneration of the American cities, and, given the continuing conservatism of Congress which prevents an equivalent increase in taxation, it is necessary to divert resources from the defence budget: the obvious place to economize is in the American forces in Europe. There is, moreover, a growing sense that a power as strong as the United States should not let its policy be shaped by its relations with smaller powers, and that the true exponent of the American tradition is personified not in John F. Kennedy with his unnatural Europhilia but in Dwight D. Eisenhower with his famous admonition:

> I believe we should not commit ourselves to any geographical line or tie ourselves down any other way. I do not believe we should handcuff ourselves with pre-action statements. We should be ready to act in our own interests when the time comes and in accordance with our own self-interest, enlightened self-interest with respect to the free world.[2]

American forces in Europe are reduced from over 300,000 to 50,000 with a corresponding decrease in tactical nuclear weapons and naval forces. Canadian forces have been withdrawn some years earlier and Canada has left the Atlantic Alliance since it no longer promotes her interests and is irrelevant to her security.

Yet several of the old allies in the Alliance are insistent that the structure of European security cannot be allowed simply to disintegrate, despite the fact that the stability of the Soviet–American balance makes the hypothesis of a deliberate attack on Western Europe less probable. What emerges, therefore, is a makeshift compromise. The North Atlantic Treaty is retained as a regional collective security arrangement under

[2] 5 June 1952. Quoted in Lincoln P. Bloomfield, *op. cit.*

Article 51 of the UN Charter, and this is justified to American opinion by the reminder that the United States is in a similar treaty relationship with the Latin American countries under the Rio Pact of 1947. The Atlantic Council remains as an instrument for the exchange of views among the thirteen remaining members of the alliance. But NATO is disbanded and in its place a small international headquarters is established to which British, German, Danish and Dutch forces are assigned, together with the one American division remaining in Europe, and under American command. This is explicitly regarded as a temporary measure (as indeed NATO was regarded in 1951). The purpose of this mini-NATO which might produce an integrated force of some 12 divisions (1 American, 3 British, 7 German, 1 Dutch, plus a Danish territorial defence force), stationed for the most part in Germany, is not to undertake the defence of Western Europe but to exercise some degree of control over a possible Central European crisis, to provide a framework for the *Bundeswehr*, and to offer some diplomatic counter-weight to the Soviet forces remaining in Eastern Europe. Some arrangements are also made for the co-ordination of naval operations in European waters in a crisis, although the normal level of American naval forces there, including the Sixth Fleet in the Mediterranean, is considerably reduced. The fact that France is now a neutral country which forbids military overflights by allied countries makes communications between Northern Europe and the Mediterranean more difficult.

## II

There is nothing in the history of international institutions such as NATO or EEC to suggest that they have a life of their own, independent of the interests of their component states. Indeed, there is already a fear that they are losing their vitality. So one must look for more serious objections to this model than the mere sense that it is a reversal of post-war Western history.

It is not an adequate objection to point to the cost to Western

Europe, in terms of economic and technological competitive power, of loosening the bonds of European association. For one thing, the effect might not be as serious as is sometimes believed: the great European technological firms, Rolls Royce, SAAB, Dassault; Fiat, Volkswagen, British Leyland, Philips, International Computers Limited and Olivetti, might simply do for themselves what governments have not succeeded in doing for them, that is organize markets, research and development and finance. For another, it should not be assumed that the mass of Europeans will care deeply if their countries do become rather technologically provincial by comparison with the United States, provided European governments can safeguard employment and keep American investment and ownership under control. They may feel that her technological dynamism has merely destroyed most of the natural and urban amenities of the United States, helped create a divided society, and has loaded her with a degree of global responsibility which would make the stoutest nation quail, and to which the European countries certainly no longer aspire. If Europe is the developed world, the United States is the 'over-developed world'.

The real weaknesses of a Fragmented or plural Europe concern its ability to confront a European crisis, the position of Germany, and the intra-European frictions it would generate. *Détente* in Europe has come to be regarded as the norm and not the exception, and considerations of European security which had governed so much of post-war Western policy have been relegated to a somewhat lower priority than in the 1950s and 1960s. But if this assumption is wrong and a European crisis appears, co-ordination would be considerably diminished and the number of independent decision centres increased. To that extent *Fragmented Europe* would be a Western Europe whose actions were less predictable in a period of tension, and many of whose governments (Norway and West Germany, Italy and Britain, Turkey, and the United States, for instance) would have lost the habit of close and continuous co-operation on politico-military questions, through participation in NATO, though still being nominally allied to each other. It would be a Western Europe of greater inherent friction even than the Europe of today, and it is doubtful whether it could surmount a severe crisis, created perhaps by some outburst of nationalism as much as by any Soviet action.

An equally fundamental objection is the position in which it would leave West Germany. Most of the NATO framework which provides not only reasonable security for Germany to-day, but also a broad political and military structure within which she can maintain her interests without serious fear of being accused of *revanchisme*, would be dismantled. She could not fail to provide far the largest single element in the smaller integrated force that was salvaged from the wreckage of NATO, and for purposes of propaganda it could now truthfully be described as a German-dominated organization even though its commander were still American. The hopes of a comprehensive Western European framework would have vanished. Germany would be the subject of a continuous contest for her loyalties: on the part of the United States, Britain and her immediate neighbours to retain the core of a collective security system in Western Europe: on the part of France to create a bilateral or purely continental system divorced from the Anglo-Saxons: and on the part of the Soviet Union to exchange a new relationship with herself and with East Germany in return for the elimination of what remains of the Atlantic political and military system and the total withdrawal of the United States from Europe. It is conceivable that this pressure from the East might strengthen if the Soviet Union saw Eastern European countries being drawn within the economic orbit of Germany. Since Germany would draw little political strength from a *Fragmented Europe*, she might be tempted to make her own bargain with the East. Almost beyond doubt, the force of nationalism would grow in German politics and policy, and the fact that she might have several bidders for her favours would put her in a position which German statesmen of the post-war generation have wisely tried to avoid.

But the pressures on Germany would not be the only stresses within Western Europe. France would be acting on a different theory of international relations, from any other West European power, based on armed neutrality. But France would not be just a second Switzerland in Europe, whose position is made acceptable to all her neighbours by the fact that, to all intents and purposes, she does not have a foreign policy. France is a much larger power than Switzerland; her neutrality would be based on nuclear weapons which would bring her into a relationship of deterrence and therefore potential hostility, not only with the Soviet Union but with the United States and Britain and their allies on the Continent: and she would be pursuing an active diplomacy in Eastern Europe and the developing world. Britain, which is in many ways France's natural partner in advanced technology, would find herself inhibited from pursuing this relationship in many fields by her decision to continue her nuclear and other agreements with the United States. Despite the continuation of the Franco-German treaty, consultation between France and Germany would become increasingly drained of content since there is no common European economic policy, as the politics of the two countries become increasingly nationalistic, and as France develops a special relationship with the Soviet Union. They could become more and more acrimonious as Germany remains loyal to the United States and France more and more anti-American.

Cleavages of a different sort manifest themselves among the countries that still belong to the Atlantic Alliance. For one thing there would now be a distinction between the outer and the inner club, between the eight who no longer were part of an integrated military system with the United States and the four who were, so that consultation in the Atlantic Council would become increasingly devoid of content or ridden with controversy as the eight rejoiced in their freedom to develop their own relations with Eastern Europe or the Middle East, and the four expressed their loyalty to the old concepts and their consequent greater influence with the United States. Each group would feel that the other had stolen a march on it.

But the five-power integrated system would have almost as unhappy an atmosphere: Britain, though still faithful to the idea of a collective crisis management system for Central Europe, would be concentrating primarily on the development of her relations with the English-speaking world and Japan. Germany's small neighbours would feel that this mini-NATO was, as the Russians keep saying, a German-dominated system.

There are two hypotheses that might knit the frayed ends of this *Fragmented Europe* together again; on the one hand, evidence that Germany, copying the policy and attitude of her neighbours and with a new generation at the helm, was becoming increasingly nationalist, and was preparing to withdraw from the NPT; or on the other, nationalism plus evidence that she was attempting to re-create *Mitteleuropa*, a central European bloc by the use of her very considerable economic power. There would be sufficient fluidity in the structure of European relations to make it possible to construct an *entente*, not necessarily a formal alliance, between Britain, France, Italy, Poland, and the Soviet Union to contain the Germanies, irrespective of the attitude of the United States. But this would hardly be an ideal means of rescuing Europe from the consequences of its fragmentation.

## III

If a *Fragmented Europe* emerged the effects would be felt, in one sphere or another, all round the world. But the country which might have to think fastest would be the United States, even though such fragmentation would be partly the consequence of her own policies. She would have eased her balance of payments problem and have stabilized her defence budget by withdrawing the bulk of her ground and air forces from West Germany, and running down the 6th Fleet to a small force in the Mediterranean. But these forces were part of a large collective effort in Europe whose strategic rationale might have been open to dispute but which had held out a reasonable prospect of being able to deter any level of threat to NATO Europe. The one division she retains in the shrunken system of integrated military forces in the central area would not be part of a system that could defend territory until an aggressor could be confronted with the alternatives of backing away, or facing nuclear response. Its sole purpose now would be to identify a crisis, stamp it out if it was minor or accidental, and set the alarm bells ringing in Strategic Air Command if it was not. The spectrum of deterrence would now have great gaps in it and the American element in Europe would avowedly be a hostage designed solely to speed the process of escalation to strategic nuclear war.

Would it be wise for the United States to be involved in the defence of Europe at all? Moreover, there would now be great areas of Europe, the Baltic, and the Mediterranean, where conflict might erupt for reasons outside American or European control, areas where she would have a residual commitment but no real control of the early stages of a crisis. Might she not be better advised to go beyond President Eisenhower's advice and regain total freedom of action? She could not denounce the Atlantic Alliance, partly out of loyalty to old friends, partly because it would involve a major shift in the global balance of power. Her best course would be to intensify her understanding with the Soviet Union, and to listen seriously to what the latter had to suggest about the organization of European security. Her negotiating position, however, would have been weakened by her loss of influence in Western Europe, though she might still look for some British and Scandinavian support.

The Soviet Union would watch the process of fragmentation in Western Europe with an initial reaction of intense satisfaction, not just because the West was becoming weaker but also because it was what Marx and Lenin predicted, that capitalist society would destroy itself from its internal contradictions. Moreover, many West European countries, Norway, Italy, Turkey, would now be 'Finlandized', nominally independent but open to Soviet pressure if it were exerted. Her freedom of diplomatic activity on both flanks of Europe would have greatly increased. France with her high population density and limited strategic force, alienated from her neighbours and bent only on the protection of her own soil, would not represent any serious menace to the Soviet Union and might be of some value as a technological partner, though her cordial relations with Eastern Europe might be a nuisance. All West European countries would be open not merely to Soviet but to Communist propaganda; not only about the fickleness of allies but about the contradictions of capitalist organization.

But Soviet control over Eastern Europe might be ebbing and she would be deeply concerned about the increased autonomy of West Germany, particularly if the infection of nationalism had spread there. Germany would now be the largest contributor to the five power collective defence force that remained within the Atlantic Alliance after the dissolution of NATO. Indeed, there would be a risk that instead of being controlled and contained within a large collective structure she could commit her allies to action against their will. The *Bundeswehr* would still be integrated with American and British forces, but how long would this last?

Of the various contenders for Germany's support it is true that the Soviet Union possesses the key, the power to offer either reunification or a real reconciliation with East Germany, and voices are raised in Moscow suggesting taking up a traditional Russian option, namely the development of a Soviet–German *rapprochement*. But a quarter of a century of anti-German propaganda among the Soviet people makes this a difficult course of action to contemplate: it might lead to serious trouble not only within Eastern Europe but within the Soviet Union as well.

Two other courses remain: one is the development of a coalition between the Soviet Union and East and West European states to contain Germany, as already mentioned, but the prospects would depend on the acquiescence of the major West European states, and until Germany began to exhibit aggressive characteristics they would, characteristically, refuse to co-operate. Besides such a course would mean devolving a great deal of responsibility not only on the West European but also on some of the East European countries like Poland, who would have to be brought into any *entente* or coalition as partners. It is at best a secondary alternative, particularly as the tradition of Russian diplomacy prefers a bilateral arrangement to any form of coalition.

Another alternative would be a direct approach to the United States, facilitated by growing acquaintance with bilateral negotiations on questions such as levels of strategic weapons, stability in mutual deterrence and the problem of containing China. Concessions, however, would only seem conceivable in the event that the Soviet Union felt her position threatened by the double risk of losing her control over Eastern Europe with an aggressive China pressing on her Asian frontiers. In such circumstances the Soviet Union might propose a four power security system involving both superpowers and the two Germanies. A Four Power Council would be created whose functions would be: first, to provide a framework for the co-operation of the two Germanies and to supervise them; second to inspect ceilings on the armed forces of the two Germanies; third, to ensure that neither Germany enters into alliance arrangements with other powers; and, finally, to start on the business of drafting a German peace treaty. Responsibility for Berlin would be devolved jointly on the two German governments. If the United States were prepared to disband the Atlantic Alliance the Soviet Union would be prepared to disband the Warsaw Pact (though the bilateral security treaties within Eastern Europe would, of course, be unaffected except those between the DDR and her neighbours which would be dissolved, as would the Franco-German treaty). However, the United States would be free to make bilateral arrangements with other countries, for instance Britain. The Soviet Union and the United States would each maintain one division in East Germany and West Germany respectively, under the new Four Power agreement, to supervise it, but would withdraw all other forces from the two halves of Europe.

Britain and France would heartily dislike such an arrangement, and would protest that it was a violation of the Potsdam agreement. Their protests would not carry much weight with either super-power, because France being withdrawn into her shell, Britain giving priority to her non-European interests, would not command much influence or support in the capitals of the two super-powers or in Germany. And it is conceivable that the United States might see in such an arrangement the best available alternative in a situation in which almost all alternatives were bad, even though it represented virtually total defeat of her post-war German policy. But it is a situation unlikely to arise. Whatever the pressures on the Soviet Union, and however concerned she might be at the prospect of Eastern Europe drifting out of her control, she would be unlikely to put forward a proposal which could only accelerate this process by releasing East Germany from her exclusive hegemony. The only solution she would see reason to accept would lie in an arrangement of joint super-power control over West Germany alone, which would not only be unlikely to receive American approval but certain to arouse violent opposition among the remaining American allies in Europe.

The process of fragmentation in Western Europe would be watched with mixed feelings in Eastern Europe from the beginning. Naturally, there would be increased opportunities for bilateral arrangements on trade and technology, with neutrals like France, and other countries that have loosened their relationship with the United States. It might even be possible to have joint ventures with West European countries.

But from the start most East European countries, however, would be concerned at the diminishing American presence and interest in Europe for its effect on Germany. They would also be concerned at the prospect which *Fragmented Europe* offered of a growing Soviet diplomatic and political hegemony over almost the whole of Europe, which would mean a diminishing freedom of action for themselves. Above all, they, like the smaller Western European countries, would be nervous of the uncertainty of the European system, of what might come next. If what did transpire was some form of anti-German *entente* between the major powers of East and West Europe, many capitals would feel little confidence in such an arrangement: modern European history is strewn with such attempts and they have no wish to repeat the experiments of the classical diplomacy in a Europe where nuclear weapons abound.

If the Soviet Union did propose a Four Power arrangement over Germany, their pleasure at the dissolution of the big blocs of the Cold War would be tempered: first, by the fact that most of them must still maintain bilateral treaties with the Soviet Union, and, second, by her reminder that she alone has solved the German problem, that she is the guardian of the security of Europe.

It is almost certain that most East European countries would prefer a broader European security system than one simply confined to Germany, one which involved all the major states of Central, Eastern, and Western Europe as well as the two super-powers. But this might no longer be practical politics in a situation in which co-operation within Western Europe and between Western Europe and the United States had steadily eroded.

## IV

Whatever model one constructs of a *Fragmented Europe* it proves as transitional as its predecessors. The attempt to hold together the relics of the NATO system in a situation in which most of the West European states were giving complete priority to their own affairs, can hardly be successful for more than a few years. *Fragmented Europe* would either lead back to *Atlanticized Europe*, or to still further fragmentation, depending partly on American attitudes – whether, for instance, she maintained a general interest in Europe or concentrated on bi-lateral relations with Britain and Germany – partly on developments in Europe itself. It would put a great strain upon Western

Germany, both to perceive where the balance of her true interests lay, and to restrain the force of nationalism, considered a virtue in other countries, in order to avoid ostracism. This would negate many of the advances that Germany has made over the past twenty years in acquiring a non-discriminatory position within the international community, and thus itself contain the seeds of further trouble. *Fragmented Europe* could prove a nightmare playback of European history between 1918 and 1939.

Chapter Five

# PARTNERSHIP EUROPE

## I

The last model of *Fragmented Europe* depicted a group of countries, disillusioned by their experiences during the 1960s, who had decided to go their separate ways. In the present model these same European countries are shown as having drawn different conclusions from the events of the late 1960s and early 1970s. Their objective is a federal Europe in partnership with the United States.

With General de Gaulle's departure from the scene, and mindful of the social and political upheavals of the late 1960s, France accepts that she cannot promote her interests by attempting to assert her leadership within a group of six European states which are bound together by little more than a customs union, which lacks the strength to withstand the encroachment of American industrial power or to exercise any lasting influence on American policies, and which could not, independently, protect themselves against internal subversion or external Soviet threats. The addition of British military power, technology, and markets is regarded as essential to the preservation of a West European identity. West Germany's enthusiastic pursuit of her Eastern policy in the late 1960s has been thwarted by the obstruction of the Soviet Union, reluctant to contemplate any change in her post-war position in Central Europe and made nervous by the liberalizing movement in Czechoslovakia and elsewhere. Resigned to waiting for the consequences of liberalization and economic reform throughout Eastern Europe to take effect, West Germany once again bends her energies towards building a corporate system in Western Europe, seeing in this the most hopeful means of ensuring a continuing American guarantee of Western Europe's

89

security, and American support for an eventual settlement of the problems of Central Europe. Britain's entry into Europe is sought by Germany as a means of freeing her from the competing pressures from Washington and Paris, and as helping to compensate for the reduction of the American military presence. Having finally concentrated her military resources in Europe, Britain joins the European Community system in the company of Norway and Denmark and seeks a solution to her economic and monetary problems in a West European structure in which she can find a new role, as the financial and banking centre of an enlarged Europe in close relations with the United States and other industrial countries.

Inspired by such individual but converging motives, the ten West European countries agree among themselves that Europe cannot expect to play a significant role in world affairs nor even find solutions to her own special problems, except by co-operating with, and influencing, the United States. The expectation is that American support for specific European interests will be forthcoming in return for European support for American policies. This partnership is looked upon as a complex relationship that will enable Western Europe to derive the maximum advantage from association with the world's most powerful state, an association which would, in the long term, prepare the way for a final European settlement with the Soviet Union, even though, in its early phase, it might sharpen the division of Europe.


## II


In order to become partners in their own right and to claim equality of status, if not of strength, in this new relationship with the United States, the ten European countries decide that they must construct an intimate community which will be sufficiently independent not to become a satellite, and sufficiently powerful and co-operative to sustain the role of an equal partner. This is the common goal which will allow each of them to achieve satisfaction.

Their final objective is the creation of the United States of Europe. This is a federal structure, with a federal parliament and a federal government to which the component states surrender powers of decision in the fields of economic, monetary, defence, and foreign policy. But it cannot be created overnight. West European Governments direct their countries along the road to federation. They build upon the common institutions of the existing European Communities; first developing the power and scope of the economic union based on the three fused Communities of the Treaties of Paris and Rome; increasing the area of functional and technological cooperation between the federating states; gradually transferring powers of control to a federal Parliament; and aiming eventually at a merging of their economic, military, and political powers in the constitution of a federal super-state.

Several collective ventures are launched: including a European Industrial Reorganization Corporation (EIRC) to promote mergers across national frontiers, and the formation of powerful European groups in the advanced industries; and a European computer, electronic, and communications agency (ECECA), designed to create a common market in public buying and development contracts and a common telephone and communications system for Europe.

At an early stage in the process of federation the West European governments, faced with a substantial reduction by the United States of her military presence in Europe, set about the construction of an integrated European Defence Community (EDC). In contrast to the European Defence Committee, which forms part of *Evolutionary Europe*[1] and which is essentially a non-operational mechanism without its own command structure, the EDC of federating Europe is conceived at the outset on supranational lines. It comprises the following elements: a European General Staff with integrated

[1] Not to be confused with the plan for an EDC conceived in the early 1950s.

planning staffs, the integration of national forces at divisional level, standardization of equipment and methods of training, and a single European logistics system. Within the EDC there is a European Defence Commission with its own budget, to which member states contribute fixed proportions; and a European Arms Development and Procurement Organization for all major weapon systems.

In the first stages of the EDC's construction, the residual British and French nuclear forces remain outside the EDC system under national control, representing national defence insurance policies without any European pretensions. If, however, they have been maintained and still represent a significant military potential when the Federation's political and defence structure is nearing completion, they will have to be absorbed into the EDC. Federal Europe, as the 'successor' state to Britain and France under the terms of the NPT, will then have to decide whether to maintain its own strategic nuclear force.

At first the basic structure of the Atlantic Alliance is retained, but a special system of consultation and joint policy-making is developed for the purpose of co-ordinating European and American policies, both within the Treaty area of the Alliance and, to a lesser degree, outside it. Unless, or until, federating Europe has taken the decision to maintain its own strategic nuclear force, American strategic power is accepted as the single and comprehensive deterrent force of the partnership. To give credibility to this, American troops continue to be stationed in Europe for the time being. Machinery is set up for crisis management, combining a system for contingency planning with a planning centre in Washington for co-ordinating the political views of the two partners about likely crisis areas. In the early stages, the ten component states of the future Federation retain their separate identities and representation in NATO. Their influence on American policies increases to the extent that they are able to present a collective European view, derived from their efforts in the European Council of Ministers to harmonize their external policies and from their integrated planning within the EDC system. As the Federation crystallizes they are progressively able to speak with a single voice and become a significant element in the policy-making machinery in Washington.

Already at this stage the component states of the future European Federation are sufficiently unified and identifiable as a distinct power group, principally concerned with Central European problems, to justify a special relationship with the United States within the NATO Council. During this formative period, the forces of the EDC are assigned to NATO and a number of senior NATO posts are filled by EDC representatives, rather than by representatives of the ten federating states. There is a Supreme Commander for Europe (the area of the ten countries, excluding Greece, Turkey, and Portugal), who is a European, with an American Deputy responsible to the President for the control of American nuclear weapons in the European theatre.

As the Federation nears completion so the pressure grows to transform the Alliance, originally conceived as a multilateral collective security system, into a new bilateral relationship between the two industrial super-states of the West, in which the other members of the original Alliance, Canada, Portugal, Turkey, Greece, and Iceland would be offered bilateral defence treaties with each of the partners.

## III

The model has two special features. First, it has distinctive historical overtones. It bears a close resemblance to the ideal association of an equal partnership between Western Europe and the United States proclaimed by enthusiasts on both sides of the Atlantic for the past twenty years. Though lately out of fashion, it still officially represents the ultimate objective of policy for the United States and the NATO governments in Europe and even President de Gaulle has, from time to time, subscribed in theory to it. It was a central feature of President Kennedy's 'Grand Design', whose classical formulation was first given in his Independence Day speech at Philadelphia in 1962 and more succinctly a year later in Frankfurt, and whose symbols were the 'twin pillars' and the 'dumbell'.[2]

The idea must remain predominant in American policy, if the concept is to prevail in the 1970s. It assumes that the United States, far from having lost interest in Europe, is willing to make the effort necessary to sustain a relationship of co-operation with a powerful, though junior partner; and that this is a deliberate preference over either a weak and subservient Europe (*Atlanticized Europe*) or a stronger but uncooperative Europe (*Independent Federal Europe*). The motives behind this choice may be various, but they include the following: (a) the need to secure a more equitable sharing with Western Europe of the military burdens of the Alliance, and of the global responsibilities of the United States in assisting the developing countries of the Third World. This motive becomes the stronger the more the United States is worried by her own domestic troubles and monetary problems. As the Americans find their imperial role increasingly irksome, they look to Western Europe to share more of the obligations, as well as the odium, of world leadership; (b) the belief that a powerful, united group of nations in Western Europe will act as a counterweight to the influence of the Soviet Union and relieve the United States of her commitment to station a large number of forces in West Germany; (c) the expectation that a West European federal structure will not only reduce the risk of the United States becoming involved for a third time in wars between the nations of Western Europe, but will also bind Germany permanently into the Western system and prepare the way for an eventual solution to the German problem; and (d) the realization of the need to accommodate a powerful commercial competitor or confront an increasingly embittered

[2] Only a Europe united and strong could function as 'a world power capable of meeting world problems as a full and equal partner. . . . With only such a Europe can we have full give-and-take between equals, and equal sharing of responsibilities, and an equal load of sacrifice' (*Department of State Bulletin*, 22 July 1963), p. 118.

relationship with Europe. In short, the United States is encouraging the growth of a strong, united Western Europe
which, in times of tension, will contribute significantly to the
security of the West and, in times of *détente*, will provide a
satisfactory framework for Western Germany and help towards
a settlement in Central Europe; while sharing some of the
global burdens and responsibilities.

The other special feature of *Partnership Europe* is that it is
essentially an organic structure, evolving from its earlier form
of economic and technical co-ordination, through the creation
of new supranational institutions, to its apotheosis in a United
States of Europe. Unlike the succeeding model (*Independent
Federal Europe*) it has two facets: the federating stage and the
completed Federation; the formative phase and the finished
product. It is useful to keep this distinction clear, since it is
precisely during the transitional period that the points of strain
are likely to emerge, both within federating Western Europe
and between it and the United States.

The first question is whether the initial impetus to create the
United States of Europe can be preserved; and at what stage
the points of maximum tension are likely to be reached. It is
not convincing to assert, with the present day Eurocrats, that
only the Community method can provide the driving force
required to sustain a steady movement towards full federation;
and that the whole process then becomes inevitable by virtue
of the pressures generated by the very mechanism of the
Community system.[3] Economic co-operation is not the only
road to political unity and there can also be different structures
for the economic, monetary, defence, and political sectors of a
federating Europe. Although, in the model, the West European leaders have elected to build initially on the existing

[3] 'We have created an organism which, by virtue of its design and of the
questions and challenges it constantly produces, confronts those who bear
responsibilities in Europe with a continuous series of situations and options
to which, if they are guided by reason, they can only respond by further
unification of Europe.' Dr Walter Hallstein's Speech to the Federal Council
of the European Movement in Rome on 20 January 1968.

community structure, they will most probably have to go beyond this at a fairly early stage in order to keep up the momentum towards the final goal of a European federal state and to overcome the resistance to unification, which will increase with the further demands for surrender of national sovereignty. The more the process of unification is extended into such jealously guarded realms of sovereignty as taxation and incomes policies, and beyond into the hallowed sanctuaries of foreign and defence policy, the less adequate will the community method appear to be as a 'federalizing' instrument. This may be particularly important in the construction of a European Defence Community where the basic problem of 'federalizing' is most graphically illustrated, namely the moment when the separate nation states are called upon to relinquish their sovereign right to take their own decisions about their own security.

There are several interesting questions here. Can defence play a role in the process of European federation? Can a European Defence Community be fashioned before there is a political structure to control or match it? Or can such integration in the defence field even act catalytically as a federating impulse?

The experience offered by the abortive EDC in the early 1950s[4] must be seen under the special circumstances of that period – Stalin's militant policies, the Berlin crisis and the Korean war, and the accompanying pressures for German re-armament. Without a set of similar crises or pressures, which will reveal the weakness of a system of separate European national defences, it is doubtful whether there can be much progress in constructing an EDC in the 1970s except as the result, rather than the cause, of a process of political and economic federation which is already under way. West European forces

---

[4] Originally conceived as a French response to a sudden American demand for a measure of German rearmament, it took the foim of a highly integrated organization for European defence and arms procurement, with an important provision for the creation of a federal political structure, based on the principle of the separation of powers, and on a bicameral system of representation.

will by then have been equipped with several generations of weapons on a national basis and it may have become increasingly difficult to evolve a common procurement system or a common tactical doctrine.[5] The longer the delay the more difficult the task. The interests of American companies in the high technology industries will become more deeply rooted, and it will be harder to obtain coherent answers from the ten countries about how to deal with this problem. In addition to the incentives of the larger European market for their defence industries and the collective desire to withstand American industrial encroachment, the European governments will also have had to reach a high degree of harmonization in their defence and foreign policies before they can make real progress in pooling the development and procurement of their advanced weapons.

While it may be possible to begin constructing an EDC without a central political authority, the crucial moment will come when national budgetry control and parliamentary scrutiny has to yield to a federal budget and a federal parliamentary authority. The final surrender of the right to declare war and to make or break alliances, which are traditionally regarded as the first prerogatives of the nation state, will probably be postponed until the federation is completed, even though the participating states may long since have lost the effective capacity to act alone. By that time, too, there will presumably have been extensive harmonization of the treaty commitments of the member states of the federation (for instance British and French membership of SEATO) and, in some cases, their re-negotiation or abandonment.

All this will take time. In the absence of some cataclysmic event which might impel the West European states to achieve their federation in one rapid stroke, the impulses which are moving them towards a United States of Europe are likely to be slow and fitful. Centralizing forces will have to contend

[5] Alastair Buchan, *Defence, Technology and the Western Alliance*, No.6, *The Implications of a European System for Defence Technology*, p. 18 (London: ISS, 1967).

with centrifugal tendencies towards separateness of the constitutional states in the federation. Diverging economic interest, dissimilar social institutions, differences in religion and language and in national characteristics, will make for the preservation of national loyalties during the formative years and will continue to have a weakening effect on the authority of a European Federal government when it is finally established. Despite the example of Switzerland, the need to accommodate at least seven different languages will be a formidable obstacle to the development of federal institutions. Indeed a form of federalism which was valid for small emerging groupings in the New World, with no history of their own and alike in language, culture and religions, is unlikely to be applicable to the old European nations with their diverse histories and preoccupations.

The federalizing movement will be constantly at risk, since it will depend on each of the component states remaining steadfastly dedicated to the ultimate objective of surrendering part of its national identity in order to gain the benefits of a wider allegiance. And since each state, as the model shows, has originally been inspired by different motives in seeking this objective, the West European federal structure will be a fragile affair during this formative phase.

Successive governments in Britain, France, and West Germany will have to convince their electorates that the goal of federation is worth the effort and the sacrifices. Each component state will be under pressure to find alternative ways to satisfy its national requirements. The citizen of this European Federation will have to think politically as a European without looking at European issues from a particular national angle. To achieve the necessary degree of loyalty and legitimacy something like a national 'European spirit' will have to be fashioned. Indeed, it is probable that, in order to hold together, the European Federation will call for a more intense nationalist ideology than exists today among the separate nation states. The United States of America, it has been pointed out, requires just such an intense ideology for its own cohesion, although its ethnic and regional differences are not nearly so deeply rooted as they are in Europe.[6]

This problem will become particularly acute if federating Western Europe were to acquire its own nuclear force, by inheriting and amalgamating the British and French nuclear forces existing at that time and then maintaining and modernizing them.[7] This is the most awkward part of the model. We have hitherto assumed that, at least initially, the British and French nuclear forces are not absorbed in the EDC and that federating Europe relies on the American strategic deterrent. But how will the British and French nuclear forces be disposed of? Would the problem of controlling them provide the final impetus to accelerate the creation of a strong federal political authority? Or would their existence prove to be a serious obstacle to Britain and France joining the movement in the first place? It is difficult to imagine a post-de Gaulle French Government, other than a purely Communist regime, abandoning control over its nuclear forces before a federal structure has been created into which it can be fitted. It is also difficult to imagine any future British Government abandoning its nuclear force so long as France retains hers.

In theory there would be no insuperable obstacles to absorbing the two national strategic forces into the structure of a federating Europe. Provided there is no question of Britain and France sharing the ownership of their nuclear war-heads or transferring physical control over them to other 'federating' states, the NPT need not prevent the Europeanization of these two forces within a political system less centralized than a full federation. The two national forces could be made available to the European Defence Community in a system which combines residual ownership with decision-making at the centre. There could be a double-key arrangement linking the national nuclear forces to the EDC (a European equivalent

[6] See Murray Forsyth, 'The Political Objectives of European Integration', *International Affairs*, July 1967, p. 492.

[7] For a totally independent nuclear force see Chapter Six (Independent Federal Europe).

of the Nuclear Planning Group in NATO) in which the non-nuclear powers are kept fully briefed about British and French weapons and there could also be commitments by Britain and France to their European partners regarding the use of their weapons, until the Federation is completed and can, if it so wishes, assume full control as the 'successor' state to the two nuclear powers. But it would require great goodwill on all sides to operate this transitional system. Moreover, the position of Germany throughout this period is certain to be very difficult, both by reason of the implied discrimination against her and of the suspicions of the Soviet Union and East Europeans that she will be gaining access to nuclear weapons.

The answer depends on how significant in relation to the EDC, the British and French nuclear forces will be regarded in the 1970s. If the Soviet Union, for instance, has deployed such a powerful system of active air and missile defences as to make it unprofitable to maintain operational nuclear forces in Europe, then they can be treated as a kind of national ornament and the two programmes reduced to research. The military power of the EDC, itself non-nuclear, would then be exercised through its new relationship with the Atlantic chain of command (a European SACEUR with an American nuclear deputy), leaving the vestigial British and French nuclear programmes outside the system altogether. If, at a later stage, when the federation comes into being, these national programmes are still significant in terms of nuclear deterrence, and if nuclear weapons have retained their international political significance, they could become an integral part of the EDC and serve as the core of a European nuclear force.

This might, however, be the signal for the two Scandinavian members to quit the federation. If, however, the partner relationship with the United States is working effectively and the American nuclear guarantee still has credibility for Europe, the federation could either develop a strategic nuclear force whose command and control was co-ordinated with the American; in other words be content with the same limited degree of 'independence' from the American nuclear partner as Britain enjoys today; or it could concentrate on short range, low-yield, tactical nuclear weapons to cover the middle range of the spectrum of deterrence in Europe. The amount of material and financial resources devoted to creating and maintaining such a force will depend on its primary purpose; whether to develop an interdependent strategy with the United States; or simply to increase Europe's influence within the partnership by placing herself on a more equal footing with the United States in the nuclear field; or to emphasize her position as an independent ally of the United States in support of the French thesis that the vital element of uncertainty in the concept of deterrence will be enhanced by the creation of another centre of strategic nuclear power in the West; or, as some European federalists have recently suggested, to serve as a deterrent in the Third World and, in particular, against other medium-sized nuclear powers such as China.[8]

But any form of collective nuclear force, though within Europe's material and financial resources, would not be credible unless there were in being a central political authority able to take the decision to use nuclear weapons, and sufficient public confidence in, and loyalty to, the Federation, surmounting separate national interests and enabling it to endure a confrontation with a nuclear adversary. This larger loyalty might take several generations to develop, but it would seem to be an essential requirement before Federal Europe could act as a fully responsible partner in a major world crisis. A great deal would thus depend, in the first instance, on the attitude of the United States. This is such an intractable problem that one can sympathize with those European federalists who hope that it can be postponed until obsolescence of the two national nuclear systems and the successful exploitation of the *détente* between East and West have, between them, changed the very nature of the problems and when other considerations may have come to assume more importance than the question of decision-making in the context of a military balance of power. But such thoughts seem wishful in the 1970s.

[8] Hallstein speech, p. 20.

## IV

*Partnership Europe* will not only have to struggle with the stresses and strains of its own federal growth, but also, simultaneously, with those of its relations with the United States. The idea of an equal partnership between a 'strong and united Europe' and the United States has enjoyed a considerable vogue on both sides of the Atlantic, at least until General de Gaulle's first veto in 1963 on Britain's bid to enter Europe destroyed an essential element in Kennedy's 'Grand Design'. But even in its early days it incurred severe criticism. The more charitable pointed to the contradiction between American support for a United Europe, economically and politically independent and powerful enough to share global responsibilities, and American insistence on retaining central command and control over nuclear weapons in the West. The more severe critics castigated the language of partnership as cloaking an American bid to retain hegemony in the North Atlantic world through the monopoly of nuclear armed forces. Others maintained that, although the United States might genuinely wish to see Western Europe acquire the cohesion and strength to be an equal partner, an alliance among nations unequal in power inevitably gave the more powerful nation a decisive voice in determining the policies of the Alliance and that this fact of political life could be obscured but could not be eliminated by talk about equal partnership. Meanwhile, Jean Monnet, a champion of the ideal of a federated Europe in an equal partnership with the United States, continued to argue that such a relationship must also be applied to the common defence and that this called for 'the organization of a European atomic force, with Britain, and in partnership with the United States'.[9]

Despite the setbacks of the 1960s and even General de Gaulle's second veto in November 1967, the concept of Atlantic partnership has survived as one objective in American policy. The familiar language appeared again in the statement

[9] *New York Times*, 18 April 1963.

by Mr Rusk in December 1967, that some new form of European Defence Organization would be welcome in that Europe might treat with the United States 'as a full partner in a reconstituted alliance'; and the US representative to the European Community later declared that 'we seek and have sought for fifteen years a partnership with a United Europe'.[10]

But the setting for an Atlantic Partnership in the 1970s will be changed in several respects. First, the American concern for West European unity is likely to decline. Her interest in Europe, it has been said, will only revive when the Europeans themselves do something interesting. There are signs of increasing American exasperation with the apathy in Western Europe and a growing desire to deal directly with the Soviet Union. The motives, part idealistic, part security, which inspired the original 'Grand Design', have lost their driving force, even though the language of official American policy may not have changed. In particular, the original American urge to unify Europe in order to supplement Atlantic defences against a Soviet military threat is already much diminished. The United States is seemingly intent on reducing, though not liquidating, her military presence in Europe.

The second identifiable change is the corollary of the first. The impetus to establish an independent Europe in association with the United States is now more likely to be European than American in origin, even though it may, paradoxically, acquire an anti-American flavour.

The third change is perhaps the most fundamental. West Europeans are thinking less in terms of their own security and of the Atlantic relationship, and more in terms of finding a mutually satisfactory relation with Eastern Europe and the Soviet Union, which may in the course of time lead to a settlement of the German problem.

What will be the impact of these changes on the concept of Partnership? Perhaps the first question is whether the assumption of many Americans and European federalists in the 1960s

[10] R. Schaetzel, Address to American Business Man's Club, Bonn, 20 March 1968.

will still seem valid in the 1970s – that the more integrated (federalized) Europe becomes, the more powerful and, consequently, effective and responsible she will be as a partner to the United States. It has been a characteristic American belief that unity is a power for good; that an integrated Europe will be outward-looking, a less cohesive Europe more parochial; and that a Europe with federal institutions would naturally become a loyal partner of the United States, whereas a Europe organized differently would remain a burden or even turn into a rival.[11] Sheer size, it seems, carries with it a greater sense of responsibility and involvement in world affairs. This is the analogy from physics – the larger the mass, the greater its impact on its environment. There is also the sociological analogy, derived from the old Hamiltonian argument that the larger the community the more secure and prosperous and therefore the more stable it will be. Thus Western Europe will behave better if it is bigger.

There are several doubtful propositions behind this assumption. There is no *a priori* reason why a stronger, united and more prosperous Europe will behave more nearly in accordance with American hopes than Europe in her present condition. A new nationalism on a European scale will not lead to closer Atlantic co-operation because Western Europe becomes larger and more integrated. The very feeling of 'European-ness', a new nationalism on a European scale, will tend to make Europe draw away from the United States. In the history of nations a separate identity has usually been established in opposition to, not in association with, a dominant power. Indeed, some Americans have concluded that Europe's political unification is likely to be born of rivalry with the United States and that this will set up divisive strains hardly conducive to partnership.[12]

[11] Henry A. Kissinger, *The Troubled Partnership* (New York: McGraw-Hill, 1965), p. 36.

[12] Lincoln P. Bloomfield, *Western Europe to the Mid-Seventies: Five Scenarios* (Cambridge, Mass: Center for International Studies MIT, 1968), p. 28. Also Herman Kahn and William Pfaff, 'Our Alternatives in Europe', *Foreign Affairs*, July 1965, p. 596.

Federating Europe's tendency to turn to independent policies will certainly be strong; but so also will remain the common Western heritage and the common interests of the two partners. Much will depend on whether the partners succeed in maximizing the areas of common interests and minimizing the areas of difference. This will, to a considerable extent, be determined by the extent of European ambitions within the Partnership. There are several possibilities.

The first possibility is that a united Europe will wish to make its weight felt in the world. The very size of a political-economic entity of 250 million people, geographically situated between the two global powers and with the second largest GNP in the world, would impel Western Europe to acquire world responsibilities. The parochialism which today seems to many Americans a European characteristic is partly a function of relative weakness. A united Europe will also seek to interpret her new relationship of equality in the fullest sense; not confining her interests to the commercial field, but assuming responsibilities for organizing the security of certain areas and supporting the United States in the maintenance of law and order in the world.

The second is that the West Europeans, though feeling no ideological impulsion or obligation to play such a role, will inevitably find themselves involved in situations which will have adverse repercussions on Europe's own security or prosperity unless they take some collective action; whether this is to protect European monetary or trading possessions or sources of raw materials, or merely to prevent a move contrary to their interests in the United Nations. Such 'minimum involvement' would be restricted to what was necessary to survive a crisis.

The third is that Europe, especially during the formative years when she will be preoccupied with her internal problems, will wish to limit her extra-European commitments to matters directly affecting her interests, mostly of an economic and commercial character (for example, the preservation of Europe's oil supplies in the Middle East or her trading links with Africa during a local war). She will be content to leave to her

American partner the major responsibility for maintaining world order.

If the frustrations of Vietnam and monetary crises have brought home to the United States the limits of her capacity to act alone in the world, she will be more amenable to accepting a powerful Europe as a partner. Yet her attitude would be ambivalent. While the loss of her global predominance would be most painful, a strong and united European partner could relieve her of some of her responsibilities, even if this also meant its acquiring the means of forcing her hand in certain fields. At the same time she would want to feel confident in her own strength before joining in an intimate relationship with a partner aspiring to be a world power. A parochial partner would create less trouble, but would also be less useful. The United States in the 1970s would probably still be interested in ensuring a minimum level of order in all corners of the world, and would expect a united Europe to share the same interest and make her contribution towards keeping the peace. This could put a strain on the partnership if Europe was reluctant to undertake external commitments except when her interests were directly affected.

In any case a closely knit partnership, with a defined structure and formal rights of consultation, might only be practicable for matters directly affecting the European–American area. The United States would not readily concede to Europe any control over her policies in the Far East or Latin America, even supposing that Europe was seeking new responsibilities there. Nor could the United States be cajoled into sharing her decisions and powers in many areas, though she would be obliged to do so if she needed Europe's agreement or support; for example, in the monetary field. Assuming, however, that for extra-European problems there would be no formal consultative machinery in the early days of the partnership, each partner would have to weigh the balance of advantage. For the Europeans it would be a choice between, on the one hand, dissociating themselves from a particular American policy, say in Asia, but at the sacrifice of any influence upon it and, on the other, winning a voice in the policy by showing concern for the problem in the form of an appropriate contribution to its solution. For the United States the choice would be between paying the price of co-determination in order to win the approval and support of the Europeans or preserving her complete freedom of decision and action, which in effect means the erosion of the partnership. Both parties would have to be clear from the outset that, if the concept of partnership is to prosper, both lose a good deal of freedom of action. This may in turn pre-suppose a fairly static international order.

The balance of choice would be especially difficult in defence matters. What would be the minimum European demand to maintain its position as an 'equal' partner in the strategic field, and the maximum that the United States could be expected to concede? The question can best be answered under the two hypotheses shown in the model: a non-nuclear federating Europe or a federation possessing its own nuclear force. On the first hypothesis, the United States might be willing to accord to her European partner some degree of 'co-determination' in strategic matters relating to the security of Europe, if the Europeans pressed hard for this and were willing to make some financial concession towards the very considerable cost of the American presence in Europe. Consultation with the Europeans about forces, weapons and the strategic concepts of these forces could be pushed much further than at present, in proportion as a coherent European view emerged, together with European organizations that could take effective responsibility.

The United States would not, however, concede similar rights of co-determination over that part of her strategic force earmarked for deterring China. And this could prove awkward. Since American strategic thinking has to be in global terms, it will be less practicable to hive off any segment of the strategic forces for special treatment and 'co-determination' with a European partner. Thus if Europe were slow to unify itself, the strategic partnership might only become feasible when its possibilities were already receding.

The second hypothesis – a nuclear Europe – poses again the question whether the United States would set her face against another centre of nuclear power in the West, or whether she would be prepared to help her European partner develop a 'junior' deterrent. The United States would be in a dilemma if the Europeans pressed for American nuclear know-how or hardware in order to maintain their deterrent in the interests of the partnership. To deny such assistance might be tantamount to denying the partnership itself and to refusing to a united Europe what had previously been granted to one of its constituent members. A key factor would be the state of Soviet–American relations at the time, and whether the United States had been responsive to any Soviet pressure to prevent federating Europe from developing its own strategic nuclear potential.

In an ideal relationship based on common objectives and mutual trust, the concept of equal partnership could safely be extended into the nuclear field. The United States would be the more willing to help a powerful European ally develop its own nuclear force if this was clearly the only way to absorb the 'independent' French and British nuclear forces, or to ensure the political stability of a united Europe, or to enable Germany to join a European federation without a sense of frustration. She might even come to welcome an autonomous centre of power in Western Europe capable of safely relaxing the demands made upon her. Or there might be some division of labour; federal Europe, though still continuing to rely on the American strategic force, might deploy a limited nuclear weapons system in support of the federation's substantial conventional forces, thus enabling the United States to reduce her physical presence in Europe. A number of American analysts, admittedly outside government, have considered that the United States was unnecessarily dogmatic on the question of centralized command and control in the 1960s. The next decade might well witness another shift in strategic policy with the Americans positively encouraging the West Europeans to create their own deterrent so that the United States, partially relieved of the burden of defending Europe, would be free to concentrate on the problem of the Pacific and her own domestic difficulties. This still appears to be the abiding hope of Jean Monnet and the European Federalists. One eminent American futurologist now argues in favour of a European nuclear 'strategic defence community' which would not only provide a 'plausible theory of deterrence and security' in the face of likely threats of the future, but would also, by equipping a unified Europe with the attributes of a super-power, oblige the United States to share her global responsibilities, thus saving the Americans from illusions of grandeur and megalomania.[13]

Despite these optimistic aspirations, it is not easy to imagine such a halcyon relationship in any future association between the United States and a united Western Europe. A European nuclear force which endowed the European partner with a measure of real independence of choice in a crisis could hardly fail to create tension and distrust within the partnership, for Europe really would possess the power to commit the United States to nuclear war. There would be a constant temptation for the United States to try to exert control over the European strategic capacity. Indeed, in examining a similar model, it has been predicted that the United States partner would secretly have to target American missiles to cover the principal bases of the European nuclear force.[14] Moreover, the Americans would face a further dilemma if there were a serious deterioration in East–West relations and a return to the conditions of the cold war in Europe. The greater the Soviet military threat the more the United States would need a strong European partner; but the less she would feel able to concede to Europe a voice in decision-making, because a unified strategy, centralization of command and quick decisions would then be at a premium again.[15] The tug of such dilemmas could become a built-in frustration to any partnership. The stronger Europe became and the tighter its federal structure, the more insistent it would be on participating in all strategic decisions. As the nuclear example indicates, the major problem of the Partner-

[13] Herman Kahn, *op. cit.*      [14] L. Bloomfield, *Scenarios*, p. 63.
[15] Arnold Wolfers 'Integration in the West. The conflict of Perspectives' in *The Atlantic Community, Progress and Prospects* (New York and London: Praeger and Pall Mall, 1964), p. 252.

ship will be that of balance. Federal Europe, though a formidable economic and technological power, could not hope to acquire in the foreseeable future the degree of strategic power, the diversity of interests or the global political influence of the United States. Her influence within the partnership would, no doubt, vary considerably; more on economic and monetary policies than on defence (unless she developed her own strategic nuclear force), more on Middle Eastern and African questions than Asian. The partner relationship itself would have an economic, monetary, political, and security content; and each would differ in breadth and intimacy, and change with the changing international scene. Thus in the monetary and commercial fields Europe would probably be enmeshed in a larger financial and trading system, embracing Japan and other highly industrialized countries and cutting across any exclusive Atlantic relationship.

Whatever her influence Europe would have to accept the role of a junior partner. This basic inequality would constitute a germ of disunity within the partnership. Europe would be sensitive to American superiority. A considerable amount of patience, goodwill, and restraint would be required of the senior partner, especially while the federation was forming and when the Europeans would be preoccupied with their internal problems and unwilling to assume new responsibilities. The feasibility of this model would, to a large extent, depend on the readiness of American official and public opinion to treat Europe like an equal partner, notwithstanding her inherent inequality. There could be no pre-ordained harmony.

The relations of Germany and Austria-Hungary, on the one hand and of the Soviet Union and China on the other, are not encouraging precedents for this. It is intrinsically improbable that harmony could be maintained indefinitely between two powers of the size of the United States and the United States of Europe without some external threat, or the presence of a third power, to help promote compromise. Once the harmony was broken, it could not easily be restored. The risk of divorce would be permanently present. It would not be enough for the two partners just to pledge their loyalty to each other, or exchange guarantees of mutual assistance.[16] It would require constant effort to overcome basic discords and to find and extend an identity of interests and aims.

What would determine whether the relationship could work successfully or not would be the depth and extent of the inter-penetration of the interests of the two partners; especially in the monetary and economic fields. There would be need for new machinery to minimize the differences and maximize the common interests. The object would be to encourage daily interchanges on major questions of policy, a habit of consultation at different levels so that the two partners could follow common policies from the outset rather than try to reconcile their differences once the crisis is upon them.

The system of consultation and joint policy-making would have to take account of these difficulties. In the field of security and foreign policy the prescriptions for effective 'crisis management' would have to be scrupulously followed – continuous discussion and defining of the political objectives which the partners should pursue, the forms of strategy most likely to keep the peace, comprehensive exchange of intelligence, in addition to a highly articulated system of contingency planning.[17] There could be a High Council at ministerial level or a 'Committee of Entente' where federating Europe and the United States government would be represented on a footing of equality, and where European and American views would be exchanged before decisions were taken on major questions of common concern such as the international monetary system, balance of payments, capital investment, technological exchanges, and aid to developing countries.[18]

[16] 'A partnership is a natural result of a common action by people who share common goals. It cannot be an image, a credo, towards which dissenting parties are pushed by force, to which sceptical believers pay tribute, only to sin against it in private.' Alessandro Silj, 'Home Thoughts from Abroad', *Interplay*, August/September 1967, p. 57.

[17] See Alistair Buchan, *Crisis Management. The New Diplomacy* (Paris: The Atlantic Institute, 1966), pp. 40 and 60.

[18] See *Resolution on the Establishment of a Relationship of Equals with the*

But one has only to describe the machinery necessary to make the model work, to see how Utopian it is. It would require a revolutionary change in American attitudes; in particular indeed in American constitutional practice. The testing period would be in the early years. The United States might not be prepared to make the necessary concessions in circumscribing her freedom of action before Western Europe had reached a high level of unity and strength; by which time the Europeans might prefer to go their own way. While for its part, Western Europe, in the throes of federalizing, would probably manifest a spirit of extreme caution. It might appear to be an irresolute partner for the United States, exhibiting all the frustrations and impotence characteristic of a confederacy in the process of changing into a federation. The historical examples of the weaknesses of the American Confederation in the eighteenth and of the German Confederation in the nineteenth century are reminders that 'by joining in a mere political confederacy nations may lose enough of their sovereignty to be hampered in their independent decisions and actions, but not gain enough single-mindedness of purpose as a group to become capable of forceful common action'.[19]

The changes in the Atlantic defence system would raise other problems. The model describes how the EDC would be fitted into the NATO structure until the alliance, in the form of a collective security system, was ready to be transformed into a bilateral relationship between the two super-powers of the West. The first casualty would be Canada. She would gain little by signing a bilateral defence treaty with the new Europe and her contemporary policy of calling in the old world to redress the balance of the new would be in jeopardy. She

---

*United States*, 13th Session of the Action Committee for the United States of Europe, Brussels, 15 June 1967.

[19] A. Wolfers, *op. cit.*, p. 239. This phenomenon can be observed today in respect of the six EEC countries whose individual activities are made less effective by their obligation to co-ordinate commercial and monetary policies within the Common Market. See also Miriam Camps *What Kind of Europe* (Chatham House Essays No. 8), (London: Oxford University Press, 1965), p. 71.

would probably withdraw her forces from West Germany and reduce her interest in central European problems, while retaining purely cultural ties with the French and British states within the federation. But the most awkward problems would arise over Germany, especially during the period of transition from the NATO/SHAPE structure, in which the German army was anchored and American influence predominant, to the new bilateral relationship replacing the multilateral one where the German component would be one of the most powerful in the EDC.

The question of the American military presence in Europe would have to be settled in a new context. Domestic pressure to withdraw her troops might be generated in the United States by the creation of the powerful European Arms Development and Procurement Organization, capable of denying the Americans the opportunity to sell arms to Europe so as to offset the cost of maintaining forces there. Or if the partnership flourished, and with it a deepening of mutual trust and identification of interests, the commitment of the United States to the defence of Europe might be so evident and convincing that the physical absence of her troops from Europe would be of little consequence. Developments in weapon systems, communications and mobility might also by then have reduced the importance of the 'military hostage' as a factor in European calculations.

On the other hand, the prospect of American withdrawal might prove to be one of the most effective impulses towards European federation. Or the very success of the federating movement might give the Americans pause. With the appointment of a European SACEUR and with Europe developing a powerful EDC, especially if it also inherits or acquires its own nuclear armoury, the United States might consider that she could no longer control the situation in Central Europe and that her European commitments were consequently at risk.

However smoothly the machinery of partnership was working the United States would wish to ensure that she could continue to control the situation in the event of a crisis, for example, over Berlin. In the final phase the legal position on Berlin would certainly become very complicated. Would Britain and France retain their residual sovereign powers relating to Germany and Berlin once the federation had been formed? Or would the new federal government take them up? Or would these powers be tacitly allowed to lapse? There might well be the risk of the Potsdam agreements breaking down unless the Russians were prepared to re-negotiate them or accept a legal fiction enabling British, French, and American troops to continue to protect Berlin.

## V

How would the Soviet Union and the East Europeans react to the phenomenon of a unifying Western Europe in intimate association with the United States? One could easily imagine two contrasting situations. In the first, the Soviet Union is increasingly preoccupied by her own internal problems, her waning influence in Eastern Europe and the mounting threat from China. The greater the Chinese threat the more the Soviet leaders are obliged to tolerate the liberal movement in Eastern Europe. They no longer feel that time is on their side. They are, therefore, willing to make concessions to promote a European settlement in order to ensure that the Americans and West Europeans do nothing to exploit the Soviet Union's weakening position. In the second, the conservative successors to Brezhnev and Kosygin, determined to correct the errors of their predecessors, are concerned to maintain the supremacy of the Communist Party and ideological conformity. A relaxation in Sino-Soviet tension, following the death of Mao, also enables them safely to tighten control over Eastern Europe. The Soviet government feels no immediate compulsion to alter the political or military balance in Europe.

The second of these situations may be the more realistic, at least in the short term. West Germany would not initially have set out on the road to federation if she had not begun to feel thwarted by the Eastern reaction to her *Ostpolitik*. Moreover, the ten federating countries are seeking a partner relationship with the United States in their belief that this will eventually lead to a final European settlement with the Soviet Union, even though, in its early phase, it might serve to sharpen the division of Europe. It would be unrealistic to suppose that the West Europeans would have begun their federal movement unless they believed that a united Western Europe would help advance a European settlement, and saw no other way to achieve it. But they might well have been deceiving themselves.

Certainly opinions differ widely on this question today. European and American federalists have consistently maintained that a federating Europe in partnership with the United States, even if endowed with its own nuclear force, would mark a step towards mending the division of Europe. The classical argument is that by integrating Germany in a politically united Western Europe Soviet anxieties about Germany's position will be allayed and the Soviet Union will be prepared to allow the reunification of the two Germanies. This is still apparently the official thesis of the United States government.[20]

The argument can be stated more winningly. Would not the Soviet Union prefer to see a Germany effectively integrated in a strong West European political-security structure in which German ambitions could be safely absorbed, than to see a weak Western Europe dominated by a strong Germany, or the latter pursuing an independent nationalist policy? Moreover, East Germany could, in time, safely be integrated in a federating Europe where the political pressures for a single German state would be attenuated since 'national' weight would be decreasing in importance within a federal system.

[20] 'The United States sees not the slightest conflict between a united Europe and *détente*, including the re-unification of Germany . . . a progressive and uniting Europe should be an inevitable attraction to the East, both in economic and political terms. A Germany re-unified within the framework of a closely knit federal Europe should do much to remove the fears of those in the East who insist on the status quo as the only means of assuring their security.' R. Schaetzel, Address to American Business Man's Club, Bonn, 20 March 1968.

The opposite view is usually advanced by students of Soviet policy. The Soviet Union has always mistrusted any form of supranationalism. She has opposed integrating movements in Europe, whether in the West – the Marshall Plan and the EEC – or in the East, for example the Balkan 'federation'. A federating Western Europe, with its own foreign and defence policy and closely linked with the United States, would be a most unwelcome form of West European co-operation and orientation. It would seem to the Soviet leaders as a strengthening of the capitalist world and of Western power, a perpetuation of the American position in Europe, and a return to the era of 'negotiation from strength'. It would preclude any major Soviet concessions in Central Europe, and their inevitable reaction would be to harden their own position and adopt more militant defensive policies.

An important consideration for the Soviet Union would be the attitude of the East European countries. Would they be attracted or repelled? The experts are again split into two schools; some believe in the 'mirror image': that integration in the West would produce a similar 'integration through induction' in the East and so strengthen Soviet control over Eastern Europe.[21] Others uphold the 'magnet' theory, that Western unity and prosperity would foster Eastern disunity by acting as a magnet on the more detachable members of the East European group.[22] But neither theory is convincing in itself.[23] Why should any European country wish to become more independent of the Soviet Union in order to become drawn into a large political unit in Western Europe, believed to be dominated by Germany? Nor is the 'mirror image' theory more plausible. It is improbable that the mere fact of a federat-

[21] Marshall Shulman, 'The Communist States and Western Integration', *Problems of Communism*, September/October 1963.

[22] Fritz Ermarth, *The Communists and the Common Market*, Radio Free Europe study, 11 August 1967.

[23] Pierre Hassner, 'Polycentrism, West and East: East European Implications of the Western Debates', *Eastern Europe in Transition* edited Kurt London (Baltimore: Johns Hopkins Press, 1966), p. 331. An excellent analysis of what Hassner calls 'the contrast and the symmetry postulates'.

ing Europe would lead to a tightening of bonds between East European countries, either among themselves, or with the Soviet Union. It might well have the opposite effect, and lead to an increase in individuality and diversity in Eastern Europe, each country trying to make its own deals with the agencies of the Federal Government, and with the commercial centres and industries where its interests lay.

Nevertheless, a federal Europe in partnership with the United States would offer many points of attraction for East Europeans. The Czechs and the Hungarians would experience the strongest emotional pull from a powerful Western Europe, although they would not want to join it. In the early stages of federation all East European countries, except perhaps East Germany, would as Europeans, feel a vicarious pride in the achievement of greater European independence from the influence of a super-power. Later, however, they would feel themselves excluded from the European movement while Western Europe was pre-occupied with its formidable double task of federating and of defining its new relationship with the United States. And as this process would inevitably be slow and protracted, they would have little choice but to retain close links with the Soviet Union.

As regards the partnership the East Europeans, especially the Czechs, would not want to see the American presence withdrawn to a point where Germany was left as the pre-dominant military power within a West European union. They would therefore welcome, at least tacitly, a partnership which implied a continued American military commitment to Europe. The Polish and East German attitudes would depend largely on Germany's position on re-unification once the fed-erating movement had begun. The Poles would be the most suspicious that West Germany would somehow retain *revanch-ist* aspirations, and might even transfer them to the new fed-eration. The East German reaction might be more favourable. The more the West German state was absorbed into the body politic of a European federation the easier the task of an East German government to secure international recognition as the heir to the German tradition. Thus one unforeseen result of the Atlantic partnership might be to endow the Pankow regime with the right to speak as the only 'sovereign' German state.

All these factors would affect the Soviet Union's reaction. She would be uncertain about these emerging shapes in the West; in particular, the place to be occupied by Germany in Europe.[24] Her instinct would be to oppose the creation of a second power centre in the West, however much a unified Western Europe might, at first, appear to advance the Soviet interest in freezing the division of Germany. She would try to build up some credible counter-weight in the East by reinforcing her ties with the East European countries.

But her first aim would be to disrupt or undermine the federating process in Western Europe at the very outset; at least to stop West Germany from participating. What inducements could she offer to a group of West European countries who were pursuing their objective of an intimate relationship with the United States while converting themselves into a federal state? To have any effect, the offer would have to be far-reaching, such as the termination of Europe's divisions and the removal of all restrictions on relations with Eastern Europe. This would almost certainly be too high a price for her to pay. What price could she afford to pay to prevent Germany from joining her federating neighbours? The Soviet Union would be cautious about offering any form of re-unification because of the repercussions in Eastern Europe; and because, if the two German states were brought together outside a wider framework, they might either become another unpredictable power centre at the heart of Europe, or seek to rejoin the European federation at a later date. But if the Soviet Union offered a price lower than full re-unification, such as a new system which would preserve the two separate German administrations while allowing normal contacts between the peoples in the two halves of Germany, the German government, having embarked firmly on the road to federation, would

[24] For a fuller account of this attitude see Chapter Six (Independent Federal Europe), pp. 143-144.

probably refuse it as an inadequate alternative. If, therefore, the Soviet Union were not prepared to pay a high price at the start, the price would rise as the federating movement advanced.

The Soviet Union might hope to mobilize the West European Communist parties into frustrating the process of federation, but she could not count on them. If they followed a Moscow line they would weaken their own political standing in Western Europe and, consequently, their power to influence the situation. But if they sought to ensure their political future in a united Western Europe by co-operating with the federating movement, they would drift away from Moscow and increase the multipolarity of the Communist world.

The Soviet Union would also be working to prevent the growth of a partner relationship between Western Europe and the United States. She would no doubt prefer to continue her 'limited adversary' relationship with a conservative United States, provided the latter was content not to stir up trouble in Eastern Europe, than to deal with a new, unpredictable power in Western Europe, subject to growing pains and likely to be a disturbing factor on her Western frontier. If Western Europe decided to exercise its nuclear option and develop its own weapons of mass destruction, the Soviet Union could hardly be expected to stand quietly by while the European force was being constructed. But she would be unlikely to go beyond political pressures. The Soviet Union might then offer the United States a world-wide *entente* based on a co-operative approach towards such major questions as the technological arms race, the organization of security in Europe, the Middle East and South Asia, the problems of conflict in the Third World, on condition that the United States helped prevent Western Europe from federating and acquiring its own nuclear force. If the United States were to respond she would destroy the new relation of partnership. More probably, the conditions which had given rise to the model would preclude the United States from interfering with the federating movement in Europe. But she might be faced with a tempting alternative to an objective about which she had now begun to develop some doubts.

There will be more than enough obstacles to prevent this model working at all, without the negative assistance of the Soviet Union. Nevertheless the latter's attempts at disruption might well prove ineffective since the federating movement already presupposes a significant change in the political climate of Western Europe and a far more united spirit than exists today. And this would probably surpass the traditional Soviet understanding of how to deal with smaller nations and how to manipulate the bilateral relations between them.

If then the Soviet Union failed to prevent the uniting of Western Europe or the formation of an Atlantic partnership, she would have to be reconciled to the consequences. One optimistic view is that, despite its latent instability and disharmony, this partnership between two great powers in the West would look solid enough to the Soviet leaders. It would change their expectations and put an end to a series of post-war policies and hopes for advancing the Soviet position in Europe by threatening or dividing the West. It would oblige them to take a fresh look at the problems of Central Europe and even, perhaps, to take some action to promote a European settlement. Such thoughts lead on to suggestions that the Soviet Union might feel constrained to grant the East Europeans a more effective voice in a re-organized Warsaw Pact and COMECON; or even to encourage an embryonic political union in Eastern Europe which might eventually form part of a European security system over which the Soviet Union would still be able to exercise some control. But this is to move into the dubious world of the 'mirror image', and it is still too speculative to be rewarding.

Moreover, it evades the central question – what the position of Germany would be? It may be the case that the evolution in Eastern Europe will probably not be much affected one way or the other by the Western Europe shown in this model, and that the Soviet Union could do little to smother the federation at birth and will therefore have to come to terms with it once it had reached maturity. While it is still forming however the federation will itself have introduced a fundamental change in the situation. A West European Federal State will be inheriting the unsolved German problem but it is unlikely to pursue the same Eastern policies as the German Federal Republic. Far from fulfilling the hopes of its American and European advocates that a federal Europe will provide a satisfactory framework for Germany and help towards an eventual settlement in Central Europe, a pre-condition for a European Federation might well have to be the renunciation by Germany of the goal of re-unification, and also perhaps, as we have seen, of special links between the two parts of Germany. In short, this would not be, as the model suggested, a deferred hope but an unconditional renunciation. The model would not therefore be likely to lead to a mending of the division of Europe. At best, it would leave things as they were. At worst, it would cause a hardening of the Soviet Union's attitude and a strengthening of her hold over Eastern Europe.

This is not an encouraging conclusion for those Europeans and Americans whose ideal Europe of the future is something very similar to this model. Indeed, it is surprising that it should still remain the popular ideal of so many Germans who now appear to be giving a higher priority to *Ostpolitik* than to *Westpolitik*. For it has turned out to be essentially a model of a federating Western Europe, preoccupied with the problems of its own formation and its relations with the United States and, in contrast with *Europe des Etats*, only secondarily concerned with events in the Eastern part of Europe.

## VI

The initial impulses to unification and thence federation are not easily discernible in Western Europe today. What might such impulses be? The renewal of the Cold War? Or the determination to withstand American industrial encroachment which is seen as a threat to Europe's greater prosperity? Or an upsurge of feeling amongst the younger European generation in search of an ideal and an identity? The shock of an American military withdrawal finally making Europe realize that it must unite in order to ensure its own protection? Or the unforeseen consequences of a change in the international financial system, with a new European monetary system acting as a catalyst to political unity?

Some of these forces, especially the last two, might prove strong enough to set the federating process in motion. But to sustain that process over the many years required to fashion the infrastructure of a federal state out of the component nations, with their different histories, languages, institutions, and traditions will be a truly formidable task.[25] It presupposes a happy coincidence of circumstances which will allow the West European countries, through differing motives, to find satisfaction for their national interests within a single European structure, and then not to waver. It only requires one maverick amongst the larger countries and the hope of federation would disappear.

Equally formidable, as we have seen, will be the task of maintaining the partner relationship between federating Western Europe and the United States. Could the United States exercise the patience, goodwill and restraint needed to make the partnership work? The American record in this respect is not promising. A partnership of 'equals' could only be maintained if both partners continued to act in sympathy and in harmony, so as to counter the centrifugal forces implicit in the concept of 'equality', and the constant risk of a divorce which could not easily be mended. A relationship of full equality in terms of power, in the strategic as well as in the economic field, would be destructive to this model, even if it were attainable. The central problem would be how to reach an acceptable mixture of equality and inequality within the partnership, in the absence of a third party to help adjust the balance. A state of near equality and healthy competition in the economic and

[25] See Dusan Sidjanski, 'Will Europe be united on Federal Lines?' in *Futuribles* (Geneva: Droz, 1965), p. 211ff, for a remarkable exercise in imaginative thinking on this subject.

technological sectors should be balanced by a marked inequality in strategic and nuclear power, compensated by a generous share in policy making.

This is the concept that still has the widest appeal on both sides of the Atlantic, but it would require exceptional vigilance and good luck if it is to remain stable. It would be at its weakest when Europe is passing beyond the 'Community' phase in the early period of federation. The United States would be uncertain of the speed of growth and final mutation of its junior partner throughout the awkward chrysalis stage.

*Partnership Europe* would be constantly subject to the risk of slipping back into *Fragmented Europe*, and to the equal risk, once federation is achieved and especially if it acquires its own nuclear force, of becoming an embittered association of rivals and leading into the next model of an Independent *Federal Europe*. Thus the prescription of Monnet and the European federalists for a nuclear federal Europe, as the most effective equal partner for the United States, would probably produce its opposite.

# Chapter Six

# INDEPENDENT FEDERAL EUROPE

## I

This is the most artificial of the six models: a combination, in their extreme forms, of the independent orientation of *Europe des Etats* and the final federal structure of *Partnership Europe*. Although lacking in plausibility it is worth studying because it combines two potent forces in Europe today – the desire to be independent from the super-powers and to find and assert a separate European identity – with the organized power to make a reality of both. Its chief interest lies in the problems caused by the emergence of a new European power, armed with a nuclear force of its own and in no way linked to either the United States or the Soviet Union, but on the contrary, challenging their respective positions and complicating the relationship between them.

The essential element for an *Independent Federal Europe* is a group of West European countries who have come together in order to obtain complete independence from other powers and to exert an important influence in world affairs. All other political interests are subordinated to those objectives. These European states, having realized that their aims cannot be achieved except by pooling their resources and surrendering part of their sovereign powers to a central authority, have established a West European federal state.

There are seven members of this Federation: the six original countries of the European Communities and Britain. Most models of a unified Western Europe tend to leave Britain floating in some unidentified limbo, because they assume that, unlike Germany and the others of the Six, Britain will remain, in the foreseeable future, too closely associated with the United States to be able to play a leading role in any 'third force'

Western Europe. It is certainly true that in this model British membership of the new federal state is not required in order to satisfy the same conditions as in the previous model, where the relation of partnership with the United States would have made little sense with Britain outside the European entity. On the contrary, in *Independent Federal Europe* it is irrelevant whether the United States takes a positive attitude towards West Europe's internal construction; if anything, it might be counter-productive. Britain has, nevertheless, been predicated as a component state of *Independent Federal Europe*, on other grounds. The economic, technological, and military strength and the resources, especially nuclear, needed to sustain Europe's role as an independent world power, would not be obtainable unless Britain were included. Moreover, the same motives that are observable in continental Europe are growing in Britain. The same is not, however, true for Norway and Denmark; indeed, the two Scandinavian countries would probably be loath to lose their identity in a federal state which was spending heavily on nuclear arms and aspiring to assert itself as a world power.

The federal structure adopted by these seven states is composed of three elements: (1) a bicameral parliament, with a House of Deputies representing the peoples united in the federal community and directly elected in proportion to the population of the several countries, and an Upper House or Senate representing the people of each state; (2) a Federal President elected by universal suffrage; (3) a Federal Council of Ministers nominated by the President and giving due representation to the governments of the component states in accordance with the provisions of the Federal Constitution. The Federal Government is equipped with decision-making powers and the means of conducting foreign, defence, and economic policy, including taxation. The Federal Constitution precludes discrimination against any member state or its nationals. Thus the President, Prime Minister or Defence Minister might equally be German as French, British, or Luxembourgois. The constitution preserves a careful balance between the area of states' rights and federal competence. There is a single West

European currency and a federal reserve fund. It is federal policy to raise standards of management and research and to develop European markets so as to achieve industrial and technological independence. This is supported by a strong protectionist policy, controlling the inflow of external capital.

In its external relations, the Federation's principal aim is to preserve a position of independence from the United States and the Soviet Union and to pursue its own policies towards the two super-powers, the Eastern European countries, and the developing world. When the federal state comes into existence, it inherits the French and British seats and rights, combined as one seat, in the UN Security Council. The Federation has also inherited the national nuclear forces of Britain and France which form the basis for constructing a strategic force, designed to protect all the member states in the Federation and to serve as a credible deterrent in the eyes of any power in the world. In short, the United States of Europe adopts a posture of armed neutrality.

The Federation does not succeed to the treaty commitments of its seven member states in respect of the Atlantic Alliance which is, consequently, abrogated although the United States may retain bilateral defence relations with some of the European states outside the Federation, such as Norway, Denmark, Greece, and Turkey. The unsettled German problem becomes the responsibility of the Federation as a whole. American forces are withdrawn from Western Europe with the accession of Germany to the new European federation, and all American bases in Western Europe are abandoned.

## II

The first question to ask is why such a powerful Federation should ever have come into being, with its own nuclear force, unified foreign, defence, and economic policies and its determination not to be in any way dependent on another power. The motive would have to be extremely powerful in order to overcome the age-old diversities in the history and the national make-up of the component states. In all respects the initial impulse to unification would need to be much stronger than that suggested under the previous model of *Partnership Europe*.

Such a formidable United States of Europe is not something into which these West European nations could have drifted as a consequence of their work together over the years in the economic Communities. Nor is it convincing to postulate that the search for prosperity and security, necessitating a common European foreign policy, could become a driving force sufficiently powerful to bring about such an advanced degree of European unity.[1] A stronger compulsion would be required before the European governments would be ready for this degree of unification: to bind themselves contractually to take common action, and only common action, on important questions of foreign policy.[2] A large, constructive European political act, on an heroic scale, must have taken place at some stage. The result of a traumatic shock perhaps, a great cataclysm in world affairs, the threat of a clash between the two super-powers and the risk of Europe being annihilated without being heard.

It is difficult, however, to imagine the kind of international crisis which could serve as the catalyst to produce a compulsive desire for independence as well as federation in Western Europe – the hallmarks of the model – since this would imply both a strong revulsion against the United States and, simultaneously, renewed apprehension of a Soviet threat. The fear of such a threat would be more likely to foster, not a spirit of independence, but a desire for closer ties with the United States. Nor would a renewed Soviet threat necessarily act as a centripetal force on Western Europe. It could have precisely the opposite effect, with the separate European states adopting different attitudes towards the East.

A more plausible form of international trauma, which might

[1] Michel Massenet, 'The Foreign Policy of a United Europe', in *Futuribles* (Geneva: Droz, 1965), p. 357.
[2] Miriam Camps, *What Kind of Europe?* (London: Oxford University Press, 1965), p. 116.

produce the simultaneous effects of independence and unity in
Western Europe, would be the threat to Europe of an *entente*
between the Soviet Union and the United States: the two
super-powers acting together to settle European issues without
the European nations being consulted. This could be less dramatic, but no less compelling, than a threat of a nuclear war. It
would be the realization of a fear that has haunted many Europeans, especially General de Gaulle, since the Cold War began
to recede – the reign of the two world hegemonies. Such an
*entente* is, equally, the prescription which some politicians and
writers have seen as offering the only guarantee of a world
order against the greater threat of nuclear anarchy.[3] And it is
not altogether fanciful to believe that during the next decade it
may come about: a global co-operative arrangement which
would take precedence over all other competing interests such
as the respective regional alliances of the two super-powers. It
might take the shape of the old-fashioned condominium, with
the world divided into Soviet and American spheres of influence.
Or, more hopefully, a kind of trusteeship under which the two
governments would jointly act as sponsors of international
order, finding common interest not only in avoiding wars and
controlling the arms race, but also in confronting the effects of
the world population explosion and re-imposing order in the
developing world.[4] Those who believe in this latter possibility
also believe not only that developments in military technology
will lead to something like genuine parity in destructive capability between the Soviet Union and the United States during
the next decade, but also that the men then reaching power
in these two countries will be temperamentally better fitted
to co-operate in world leadership than is the present political
generation.

Such a double hegemony might conceivably have provoked
Western Europe to react strongly enough to start building the

[3] E.g. John Strachey, *On the Prevention of War* (London: Macmillan, 1962),
p. 326.
[4] See Robert W. Tucker, 'United States-Soviet Co-operation. Incentives
and Obstacles', *The Annals of the American Academy of Political and Social
Science*, University of Pennsylvania, July 1967, pp. 9 and 12.

structure given in this model, in the hope of dividing the United States and the Soviet Union and then acting as the balancing element between them. But, by the same token, this European aspiration to be a 'third force' would have met the strong opposition of the two most powerful states in the world, whose separate strengths would now be enhanced in *entente*. Consequently, the emergence of an *Independent Federal Europe* and its bid to develop its own nuclear force would, in all probability, have been thwarted before it had got very far.

A trauma of a different kind which might serve as the sufficient cause for the genesis of this model would be the threat of a nuclear Germany. Here the setting would be different: the United States over-extended in Asia and disengaging in Europe and the imminent collapse of NATO and rising neutralism in West European countries. Germany, no longer feeling adequately protected, renounces her pledges under the revised Brussels Treaty, abrogates the NPT and starts constructing a nuclear force of her own.[5] The other West European states, scared by this prospect of a German national deterrent, decide to pool their resources and offer Germany equal participation in a European nuclear force, which thus becomes the catalyst for constructing a West European political federation. This would be re-enacting, in a nuclear field, the history of the treaty for a European Defence Community in the early 1950s, which was born out of fear of German national rearmament.

But whether the primary impulse was fear of an external or internal threat or a feeling of inferiority and insecurity, it is difficult to imagine such a West European Federation springing into life except by way of a transcendental European nationalism which, in its turn, would be largely nourished on a feeling of resentment and antipathy towards the United States. A sense of acute uncertainty about the future, combined with a conviction that the United States could not be relied upon to

[5] The practical difficulties for Germany of developing nuclear weapons and a strategy for them without the co-operation of at least some allies are immense. She has no test areas, a high population density, and a small aerospace industry.

relieve it, might conceivably generate powerful emotional forces within Western Europe sufficient, perhaps, to bring about an *Independent Federal Europe*. In such circumstances, feelings of resentment and suspicion would become mutual. The United States would not welcome the emergence of a third nuclear power centre controlled by an unfriendly Europe, and might try to prevent it. This might provoke the West Europeans to seek their own security through unity and power as a 'third force' on the world stage: 'paradoxically, strong United States opposition to European union would, in all likelihood, prove to be the catalyst the Europeans need to take a major step forward'[6] towards European integration.

There is now a good deal of speculative literature on this subject, mostly by American writers on international affairs who are Gaullist sympathizers, which looks confidently to the day when a wider European loyalty will appear that will fashion a powerful new Europe, politically united, militarily independent of the United States, nationalist in spirit, self-assertive and anti-American. One writer foresees a West European union being accomplished in opposition to the United States and as an act of self-differentiation, with the French nuclear force serving as the military basis of this European political unity.[7] Another, writing in 1963, was confident that 'the [European] Community will clearly aim at autonomy, if not independence, in the field of politico-military strategy ... Gaullism has now emerged into something broader and more up to date, that is not quite European nationalism but may become identified with a conception of "armed neutrality" between the blocs which is bound to attract support from almost all points of the political compass.'[8] Another prophesies the emergence of a 'Europe militarily independent of the United States and with the political cohesion to throw its weight around', and of a new gener-

[6] Miriam Camps, *European Unification in the Sixties* (London: Oxford University Press, 1967), p. 247.

[7] George Liska, *Europe Ascendant: The International Politics of Unification* (Baltimore: Johns Hopkins Press, 1964), p. 101.

[8] George Lichtheim, *Europe and America* (London: Thames and Hudson, 1963), p. 38.

ation of European leaders 'who are aggressive, self-confident nationalists', committed to a United Europe.[9]

But if the new generation of leaders do not turn out to be these 'aggressive nationalists', *Independent Federal Europe* will not receive much of an impulse at the start. And even if the prophets are right on that score, they are wrong in supposing that the Gaullist brand of European nationalism will lead to that larger European loyalty without which a European Federation cannot be constructed. The concept of a 'united Europe' is loosely used in Gaullist writing and is sometimes hard to distinguish from the language of the European federalists. But, in fact, the federalists and Gaullists, though some of them may agree on the objective, differ profoundly on the means of attaining it. The federalists are surely right in thinking that the desire to create a Europe, which could play a world role similar to that of the Soviet Union and the United States, leads logically to a highly integrated European super-state under a strong central government with its own nuclear armoury; whereas, in the Gaullist idea of a politically united Europe,[10] the means, which are purely inter-governmental, contradict the end, which is a Europe capable of playing a global political role.[11]

It has recently become fashionable to think that the challenge represented by American industrial and technological encroachment might provoke a European response which would break the inertia of the 1960s and set in train forces making for European integration.[12] Certainly, there is a challenge here, but the problems posed for Europe are specific and confined to certain areas requiring specific counter-measures for their solution. By itself it does not provide a sufficient reason for the construction of a Federal Europe.

[9] Ronald Steel, *The End of Alliance: America and the Future of Europe* (London: André Deutsch, 1964), p. 97.

[10] See Chapter Three (Europe des Etats).

[11] Murray Forsyth, 'The Political Objectives of European Integration', *International Affairs*, July 1967, p. 184.

[12] Cf. Jean-Jacques Servan-Schreiber, *The American Challenge* (London: Hamish Hamilton, 1968).

None of these possible motives and impulses are fully sat-isfying as explanations why Western Europe should assume a posture of federal unity and independence. Another approach, which may improve the plausibility, is to suppose that the model is the deformed product of one of the other European models which has gone wrong.

One such possibility would be to conceive of *Independent Federal Europe* as an escape from, and reaction to, the un-pleasant experiences of *Fragmented Europe*. It has, for instance, been suggested that the unification of Western Europe may come about as a 're-integrative movement', when the separate states rally to contain and absorb the unacceptable consequences of further disintegration. Such a deliberate strategy has been ascribed to Bismarck, when the lesser German states were com-pelled to seek unification around Prussia as the only alternative to the disintegration of the German political system in the wake of his bold actions in committing Prussia's military strength against Austria and then France. And France today, it is sug-gested, may have adopted a similar strategy; first, by working for disintegration in the Atlantic framework, and then by seek-ing to induce the West European states to 'rally to France's concept of European defence and unity in order to escape un-acceptable alternative prospects'.[13]

But this ingenious comparison between the genesis of the German Reich in the nineteenth century under Prussian leader-ship and the prospect of a similar unification on a European scale under French leadership in the twentieth will not really do. In the first place, it will break down so long as France is not prepared to surrender French sovereignty to a larger cause. In any case, this is not a model of a Western Europe united through the domination of one of its nation states, but of a Federal Europe in which no one state has succeeded in exerting its power over the others.

The other, more likely, possibility is to follow the pointers in the last chapter and suppose that *Independent Federal Europe* is the *Partnership Europe* that went astray. There it was concluded

[13] G. Liska, *Europe Ascendant*, p. 60.

that *Partnership Europe*, once it had achieved federation, and especially if it acquired its own nuclear deterrent, would be constantly subject to the risk of becoming a 'third force' Europe. This danger would be all the stronger if the same impulses which had helped to form the European partner in *Partnership Europe*, become the driving forces away from partnership and towards independence and rivalry. Thus, the shock of an American military withdrawal from Europe or of a global financial crisis, which had separated the European and Atlantic monetary systems, might have so embittered the partnership as to produce its opposite. The very concept of a united Europe in a *fully* equal partnership with the United States could itself have stimulated a European nationalism, requiring autonomy, power and status as ends in themselves, and including a demand that Europe should possess its own strategic nuclear force. The result could be American isolationism and European neutralism interacting on each other and producing this model.

## III

This is, in essence, a model of a Western Europe which has no preferred associates nor privileged enemies. It is a proud, assertive, suspicious Europe, dependent on no one and ready to defend itself against any threats from any quarter. It is a federal state with a general strategy of *tous azimuts*, in the political and economic as well as in the strategic context.[14]

In such a hostile world the strategic nuclear arm is, therefore, a very necessary protection for the federation. There can be no question, as there was in *Partnership Europe*, of relying on the American nuclear guarantee or allowing the British and French nuclear forces to continue to exist outside the European system as minor national eccentricities; nor is there

---

[14] *Tous azimuts* is an artillery term for a capacity to fire on any point of the compass. The French strategy of 'armed neutrality' was popularized under this title in an article by the then French Chief of Staff General Ailleret Millett in the *Revue de Défence Nationale* of December 1967.

no question even of a minimal European deterrent to supplement the far more powerful force of the American partner. In the present model Western Europe is on her own. The new federation has inherited the British and French nuclear forces and from them has constructed a single European strategic system, designed to protect all members of the federation and to be a credible deterrent in the eyes of any power in the world.

The first question then is whether, in the strategic and technological conditions foreseeable in the late 1970s, an independent European federation could command the power and resources to develop a strategic system of this kind. The problem can best be tackled in two stages. First, by analysing the contents of the nuclear dowry which France and Britain would be bringing to the federation, in terms of physical resources and deployments; second, by estimating what additional range of functions would be needed in order to protect a group of seven countries comprising a population of 240 million and covering an area of 544,000 square miles.

A pooling of the British and French nuclear forces would produce in the 1970s a higher level of European strategic force than has ever existed there before. It would comprise about 125 strike bombers of limited range (75 British and 50 French), 25 French missiles *Sol-Sol* Ballistiques Stratégiques (SSBS) with a 2,000 mile range, and 8 missile-firing submarines (4 British and 4 French); perhaps some 275 units of strategic delivery, assuming one nuclear weapon for each aircraft and one warhead for each SSBS of which about 170 might be expected to be operational at any one time. This might represent a force about one-twelfth the size of the American strategic force. The mechanics of the fusion of the British and French forces would involve the creation of joint research and development systems, integrated Anglo-French planning and operations staff, and probably two integrated commands, one for submarines (say British) and one for aircraft and SSBSs (say French).

One important consequence of this fusion would almost certainly have been Britain's exclusion from access to American nuclear missile and propulsion technology, and to satellite and other intelligence. This would have had two effects. First, Europe's ability to undertake a realistic targeting system would be significantly diminished. Second, deprived of her access to American technology, Britain would in some respects be the weaker partner, despite her broader technological base in the development of strategic systems since political isolation will have obliged France to develop skills in fields where Britain had not felt it necessary.

If these were approximately the dimensions and character-istics of the Anglo-French dowry which would form the nucleus of the Federation's strategic system, the latter would have to fulfil far more ambitious functions. To protect the integrity of the larger group of countries it would have to be considerably bigger than the combined Anglo-French forces, and it would need to have longer-range weapons to reach at least the Eastern seaboard of the United States. It might entail a force of as much as 500–600 deliverable warheads – perhaps, more, if the super-powers were to deploy BMD systems. Much of the increment would have to take the form of hardened, land based missiles, partly because there is doubt of the ability of submarine launched missiles to penetrate an ABM system, but mainly for reasons of cost. This might make it necessary to base these additions to the Anglo-French forces almost entirely in Britain since there are no very low population density areas in Western Europe comparable to North Wales or the High-lands (except a small area of northern Italy). Thus the European force would have raised awkward problems from the start.

To build and harden a system of, say, 550 units might entail costs, over and above those at present borne by Britain and France, amounting to a figure in the range of $5 billion or more which spread over five years would mean an immediate 5 per cent increase in the defence budgets of the seven member countries. This figure assumes the use of existing production lines and techniques, and considerable sums might have to be added to it for improving weapons performance in step with new technologies. If, in particular, it proved necessary to pro-duce multiple warheads (MIRV) and advanced penetration aids from European resources alone, to counter Soviet (or Chinese or American) BMD systems, the costs could go up steeply. Taking account of maintenance costs one would assume that West European defence expenditure as a whole would rise immediately above the British and French level, that is about 6 per cent of GNP, and that the British and French senators would insist that it was the other units of the Federation that increased their contributions. A European BMD system, even if it could be constructed from the technological resources Europe will have in the 1970s, might add another 20 per cent to the European defence budget; even if it were decided to forego it, there would be the cost of a greatly extended civil defence programme to reckon with.

Assuming that the seven member states were prepared to make the requisite financial sacrifices in accepting this additional expenditure, a minimum deterrent could be established, certain of inflicting unacceptable damage on Soviet and American cities. The system would not have the counter-force options at present possessed by the super-powers and would become increasingly vulnerable, with a diminishing second-strike capability, if improved guidance systems, MIRV's, penetration aids and observation satellites increase the offensive strength of the super-powers in the 1970s. Indeed, the very existence of such an independent deterrent force would probably have accelerated the nuclear arms race between the United States and the Soviet Union, each striving to contain it and to restore the balance of the bipolar world which Europe was challenging in her new role as the China of the West.

To be credible, a European deterrent would have to be accompanied by adequate conventional forces. But the burden of paying for both could lead to great strain on the economy and to public opinion demanding less ambitious defence programmes. The Federal Government's ability to maintain its independent deterrent would thus be politically at risk, a factor which might itself diminish the deterrent's continued credibility.

But the main factors affecting not only the credibility of the deterrent but the chances of the continued cohesion of the

Federation itself, would be political: the structure of the central political authority, and the degree of political unity and sense of European identity and loyalty. The European Federation of *Partnership Europe* could manage with a much lower degree of internal cohesion because of its reliance on American strategic protection. But in a federation aspiring to independence, national and regional loyalties would have to be channelled into a single European loyalty, to the extent that the French accept being governed by a German, or the Germans by an Italian, and where the interests of Turin are equated with those of Manchester, of Swabia with Flanders, or of Scotland with Provence. Only when this amount of cohesion is evident would a federation be politically viable, and an independent European deterrent politically realizable.

The wish to develop a strong independent deterrent would partly govern the shape and structure of the Federation itself. Moreover, the restrictions on transfer of control over nuclear weapons under the NPT would call for a central authority, recognized by the international community as a power in its own right; not just an advanced form of coalition or confederation. Indeed, if the sole object was to make Europe an independent nuclear power in the world, then a unitary government would be preferable to a federal.

The mechanics of nuclear defence would also condition the federal structure. The choice between a parliamentary, collegiate, or presidential type of federation[15] would not be open to the Europeans. Only the presidential form, as in the United States, would suffice. Only a popularly elected President of Europe, with powers analogous to those of the President of the United States, with undivided authority in a nuclear crisis, could wield a strategic system with full credibility. A coalition government in a federal system, as in West Germany today, or even the system of cabinet government in Britain or the triarchy in the Soviet Union, might prove wanting if subjected to such a supreme test.

[15] D. Sidjanski, 'Will Europe be united on Federal Lines?' in *Futuribles* (Geneva: Droz, 1965), p. 230.

This view is disputed by Herman Kahn, who argues that the problem of credibility could be solved without postulating a strong, central political authority if a strategy of 'controlled tit-for-tat response' were adopted. The commander of the West European strategic force would have standing orders to fire a nuclear weapon in retaliation for any similar nuclear weapon launched against Europe; he would act accordingly, within a specified time limit, unless he received countervailing orders from those constituting the higher political authority, for which a two-thirds majority would be required.[16] This is ingenuous but unrealistic, if one tries to imagine what would, in fact, happen if Western Europe were left on its own to confront a nuclear crisis in the early years of the Federation's existence. Even with a Federal President and some effective political structure, a central administration would hardly be capable of taking rapid decisions on the use of the strategic arm in defiance, if necessary, of Moscow and also Washington. Failure of complete identification among its member states, or the persistence of national distrust between them, would weaken the central authority and prevent it from developing the strategic basis of independence. Any really serious crisis would involve a high risk of one of the member states opting out and of the Federation breaking up. The creation of an independent European nuclear force might, therefore, mark the formally independent character of the Federation, but without giving it the decisive power to exercise its complete freedom of action in any crisis.

IV

But though its feet might prove to be of clay in a crisis, to the outside world *Independent Federal Europe* would still appear to be a formidable power. What would be the effect on Eastern Europe and the Soviet Union of this nuclear-armed European

[16] See Kahn, Stillman and Wiener, *Alternatives for European Defence in the next Decade* (New York: Hudson Institute, 1964).

federation, which has absorbed a strong West Germany and has inherited the German problem? Unlike *Partnership Europe* where the chief interest is in the federating process and its external effects, the *Independent Federal Europe's* point of interest lies in the reactions provoked by the existence of a new European super-state in the West. If the Soviet Union had tried to suppress *Independent Federal Europe* in its infancy, she must be presumed to have failed. In attempting to assess Soviet and East European reactions it will be useful to maintain the distinction between an independent federation that has grown from the failure of a partnership with the United States, and a federation that has, so to speak, come into existence in its own right. In both cases, however, the Soviet Union and the East Europeans would have to weigh a similar balance of advantages and disadvantages, though the mixture would be different.

The gains for the Soviet Union, and also for the East European countries, would not be negligible. First, the Federal Republic of Germany would have ceased to exist as a separate nation state, and with her would have vanished her claim to re-unification. Second, the Atlantic Alliance would have collapsed; the American military presence in Germany would have disappeared, without any compensatory or reciprocal movements by the countries of the Warsaw Pact. (This, of course, is to assume that the Soviet leaders would, on balance, prefer to see the American presence withdrawn altogether than continuing to exercise its restraining influence in Europe.) Third, the East German regime would be able to claim international recognition as the only 'sovereign' German state. Fourth, most territorial claims in Central Europe would have been eliminated since Germany would have had to recognize the Oder–Neisse Line and East Germany on joining the Federation. The position of West Berlin would be highly precarious, depending entirely on Soviet goodwill and the requirements of Soviet policy.

But despite the advantages attached to the withdrawal of American forces and the new status acquired by East Germany, there would remain, in Soviet eyes, the disagreeable prospect of a powerful neighbour in Western Europe, endowed with its own nuclear arm, free from American control and capable of asserting itself in East European affairs. Moreover, whether or not the United States might also have difficulties in her relations with this new European Federation, the Soviet leaders would suspect a tacit understanding, or even an imminent *rapprochement*, between the two capitalist super-states of the West. Economic and monetary relations across the Atlantic would feed these suspicions.

There would also be apprehensions on security grounds. Although the Soviet Union might not credit the Federation's nuclear force with much efficacy in a nuclear exchange, she would nevertheless be afraid of an economically strong German 'state' becoming the dominating element in Western Europe and gaining access to the use of the nuclear force through the guise of federal membership. A German Defence Minister would not be seen by the Soviet Union simply as a West European citizen, but rather as a German nationalist secretly planning to use the federal structure and federal power to advance German claims to the East. Indeed, there are prominent nationalistic politicians in West Germany whose writings could lend themselves to just this sort of interpretation.[17]

Nor would Germany's initial signature of the NPT, or the subsequent transfer by Britain and France of control over their nuclear warheads to a newly established federal executive, allay such apprehensions. Indeed, Soviet propaganda is already pointing out that the NPT could lead to the eventual establishment of a European nuclear force.[18] But the Soviet Union would be unlikely to react so forcibly as to declare that the participation of Germany constituted an extraordinary event that justified Soviet withdrawal from the Treaty by invoking its Article 10. She might well, however, threaten to do so, with

[17] See K. T. von Guttenberg, *Wenn der Westen will, Plaedoyer für eine mutige Politik* (Stuttgart: Seewald), 1964.
[18] Yury Zhukov, 'A Bonn-Pretoria Atomic Axis?', *Pravda*, 29 August 1967.

the double objective of aligning American policies with her own in opposition to the Federation and of convincing her East European allies that the peril of German *revanchisme* had not passed with the signing of the Treaty.

Countries such as Czechoslovakia and Hungary, who may have achieved the greatest degree of liberalization and independence, would obtain little profit. For them the continued existence of two German states, co-existing without friction and contained, respectively, by an American and a Soviet military presence, would be preferable to the disappearance of a separate West Germany and therefore the advancement of East Germany in prestige and importance. Moreover, these countries would consider that they were not only barred from joining the federation in Western Europe, but that its existence offered no compensating advantages such as helping to increase their own independence *vis-à-vis* the Soviet Union or to develop a parallel political unity in the East.

For the conservative countries like Poland and East Germany the prospects would be clearer. Poland would no longer feel inhibited by Soviet strategic requirements from asserting her own position, though she would still be dependent on Soviet military protection. East Germany, however, would have to face severe political, social, and economic reforms in order to rebuild her polity, previously conceived as the negation of the other German State, around a new objective. But it would be the East European countries who would have most to lose from the emergence of a powerful federation in the West with its own nuclear strategic system. The Federation would have the power to devastate all the cities of Eastern Europe, but it would also be more vulnerable than the American strategic force and, in East European eyes, might not be subject to the same restraints. The East Europeans would be especially fearful of Germany's role inside the Federation and its influence over the nuclear arm. The Soviet Union would exploit these fears and the result would be to reverse the trends towards reducing force levels in Central Europe or reforming the Warsaw Pact; and to cause East Europe to draw closer to the Soviet Union and for the latter to tighten its military, political and economic grip. With the hardening of the Soviet position the prospects of a European settlement would recede.

Such strong reactions could, however, be tempered by the kind of foreign policy pursued by *Independent Federal Europe*, and that, in its turn, would be influenced by the manner in which the Federation had come into existence. On the hypothesis that this West Europe is the product of an Atlantic partnership that has broken down, with all the odium of a failed political venture, the Federation's attitude towards the United States would be one of resentment and latent hostility. This would present the Soviet Union with an opportunity to exploit the Federation's urge to justify its new found independence by offering it economic and technological co-operation and access to Soviet markets, and urging the East Europeans to do the same. The Soviet Union would not have to pay any political price in the shape of concessions in Central Europe, since the Federation would no longer be relying on the guaranteed protection of a strong American partner. For the East European countries the tightened Soviet control, brought about by the very existence of a strong nuclear-armed federal state in the West, could be marginally diminished to the extent that the Soviet Union would need their co-operation to induce the West Europeans to redress their former Atlantic associations by cultivating closer ties with the East.

If, on the other hand, the Federation had reached its position as a 'Third Force' nuclear power owing nothing to either of the super-powers, and was determined to maintain its deterrent capacity equally against both of them, the situation would be different. And so would the Soviet reaction. The military aspects of the East–West confrontation in Europe would be intensified and the tightened Soviet grip on Eastern Europe would not then be modified to allow for economic and cultural links with the West. The East European countries might even be prevented from assuming separate diplomatic relations with the new Federation, and the world east of the Oder would revert to an autarchic inter-relationship under COMECON and to increasing economic, as well as military, dependence on the Soviet Union.

The Soviet Union would be probing the weak points in the new Federation; and the weakest point would be the complex of German problems, in particular, Berlin. Once the American presence and guarantee had disappeared from Europe without being replaced by a negotiated security system, insecurity and instability would have returned to the continent, with Berlin producing the likely flashpoint. The American commitment to defend Germany would have terminated with the abrogation of the Atlantic Treaty. Having withdrawn forces from Germany, she would hardly want, or be able, to retain troops in West Berlin, where they would become vulnerable hostages. The Federation would not necessarily be entitled to inherit French and British rights in Berlin. And unless the Soviet Union was prepared to allow Federal troops, or even American troops, to garrison West Berlin because this happened to suit Soviet policies, the city would be swallowed up by East Germany.

Just as, in *Partnership Europe*, unconditional renunciation of reunification was found to be a feature of German membership of a federation in partnership with the United States, so, in this model, Germany's integration in an *Independent Federal Europe* would imply her abandonment of West Berlin to East German or Soviet control. As long as Germany was free to decide its own future it would be chary of joining a European Federation of this kind. And a federation without Germany would be meaningless. The West Berlin dilemma, therefore, illustrates the unreality of this model.

One other effect, already noted, would be to stimulate co-operation between the United States and the Soviet Union in trying to keep the new Federation out of the club of the super-powers, and to deny her the balancing role she was seeking so as to avoid being played off one against the other. At the same time, 'each of the two great powers will seek either to weaken or to gain control of a new power in process of formation'.[19] The relationship would therefore be ambivalent. Both the United States and the Soviet Union would have to be careful not to drive the new Federation into the other's arms. Their co-operation would not be so much against Europe as at her expense, neutralizing her independent activities rather than opposing them. The Soviet Union would maintain a commanding position in this triangular relationship. The European Federation itself would be constantly subject either to paralysis, because of the need to preserve its cohesion by compromise between its member states, or to disintegration through threat of secession by a major state. The Soviet Union would find herself in the best position to exploit such weaknesses.

## V

In this triangular relationship the attitudes and policies of the United States and the Soviet Union towards each other and towards Federal Europe would also be affected by the latter's role in the developing world. Would the Federation's extra-European interests be limited to the protection of its overseas trade and investments? Or would the Federal Government try to gain political influence by assuming new commitments abroad? Could this new European state afford to leave it to the two super-powers to deal with the turbulence and disorders in other parts of the world without feeling some obligation to intervene?

The answers to such questions must depend on the international conditions prevailing at the time; but there are three broad hypotheses.

First, that *Independent Federal Europe* would not have the energy or the will to assume responsibilities for keeping law and order in the world; not even for the security of particular areas where traditional European interests might be at risk. Western Europe would be so preoccupied with the effort of building its new federal structure, and of protecting itself

[19] Massenet, *Futuribles*, p. 312.

and its markets against American encroachment, that it would have little left to contribute beyond a collective aid programme for developing countries. At most it would be concerned in Middle Eastern affairs, but not in the sense of military intervention. It would not become a neo-imperialist power. It would not try to regain, collectively, what its component states had lost, individually, since the First World War. The pre-war belief in the need to control the sources of raw materials would be replaced by the concept of world markets and diversification of supplies. But this hypothesis presumes an abnormally quiet world. And it is not really consistent with the setting of the model, which postulates an American withdrawal from Europe and a West European Federation which has lost confidence in the United States and seeks to assert its independence and influence in world affairs by acting as a balancing element between the super-powers. Such an American withdrawal from Europe is likely to form part of a wider retreat from post-war commitments.

Under the second hypothesis, *Independent Federal Europe* would not only be seeking to protect its security interests in Europe, but also to safeguard its growing interests outside Europe by preserving the political stability in Northern and sub-Saharan Africa and displacing American responsibility for the balance of power in the Mediterranean. If the new generation of 'aggressive, self-confident nationalists' have come to power in Western Europe, and were determined to challenge the position of the super-powers in the Third World, they would then have plenty of opportunities for doing so. They would command the resources too. Moreover, as the American concern with West European and German problems declined, the Soviet concern to widen the area of its identity of interests with the United States would probably also decline: a situation which *Independent Federal Europe* could hope to exploit. The parochialism of the 1960s, which was illustrated by the absence of any West European influence on the Middle Eastern crisis of 1967, would be seen to have been not an endemic feature of post-war Europe but only a function of relative weakness, to be corrected by a programme of strength through federal unity. This federal state, claiming to represent a European civilization which was neither capitalist nor communist, would offer the countries of the Third World an alternative way of development; and would obtain their support for her manœuvres between the two super-powers, the muscle-bound dodos of the nuclear age.

The third, more plausible hypothesis, would be that *Independent Federal Europe*, by its very size, weight and power, would incur corresponding commitments outside its own borders. Like the United States in the post-war decades, it would inevitably find itself drawn into expanding commitments, even against its own inclination. There would be the obligations and interests inherited from French and Common Market links with Africa, from the former British Commonwealth's connections and the British and French responsibilities as permanent members of the UN Security Council. Such commitments would grow as the Federation grew in strength, but their nature – whether military or political or mainly economic – would depend on how far the super-powers of that day were prepared to tolerate disorders in the Third World without feeling their own interests were at risk or trying to exploit the situation to the other's disadvantage.

## VI

The prospect of an integrated, nuclear Western Europe, pursuing policies independent of the United States – a Frankenstein monster partly created by American help and encouragement – would have troubled Americans more than it has if they believed it to be realizable. There are those who are sufficiently concerned to warn against it: 'the United States cannot rationally support a degree of political-military union for Europe which would lead to a political separation of Europe from America. . . . The American attitude on [European] political and military union ought now to be more reserved and pragmatic.'[20] But most advocates of a united Europe, on both sides of the Atlantic, hope to get the best of both worlds – a quasi-partnership relation which will fully satisfy Western Europe's search for independence while avoiding the excesses described in the present model.

Moderate European federalists believe it will be 'possible for Europe to associate some of its efforts sometimes with the United States and sometimes with the Eastern countries'.[21] Perhaps George Ball in his recent book best exemplifies this optimistic view.[22] He retains his faith in a united Europe 'as the new third super-power', which would act as a 'cushioning component' between the United States and the Soviet Union. It would offer greater scope for maintaining equilibrium than in a purely bipolar balance. The best hope for a distant European settlement would involve Americans, united West Europeans and Russians as equal negotiators.

The distinctions maintained between *Partnership* and *Independent Federal Europe* are, of course, very artificial. It would not be difficult to construct a hybrid model of a united Western Europe, independent and competitive but not antipathetic towards the United States. The concepts of Partnership and Independence are neither absolute nor exclusive. It is, moreover, unrealistic to suppose that a West European Federation would wish to pursue policies at variance with those of the United States, simply for the sake of doing so and regardless of whether or not it was in her own best interest to do so. In this respect *Independent Federal Europe* remains highly improbable. At best it is a caricature.

But it is equally true that the new generation in Western Europe might find the concept of a constitutional Federal state merely an artificial construction imposed by the European enthusiasts of the 1940s and 1950s. The new generation in

[20] Harold van B. Cleveland, *The Atlantic Idea and its European Rivals* (New York and London: McGraw-Hill, 1966), p. 162.

[21] Club Jean Moulin, *Pour Une Politique Etrangère de l'Europe* (Paris: Editions du Seuil, 1966), p. 43.

[22] See George W. Ball, *The Discipline of Power* (London: Bodley Head, 1968).

Europe may also be less resentful of American power and less willing to respond to the American challenge by sacrificing immediate benefits in order to strengthen Europe's power and independence.

But this model contains the seeds of a powerful myth; not something to be realized immediately, but a long-term hope, a distant talisman. By projecting the nation state onto the European scale and by flattering a sense of moral and cultural superiority *vis-à-vis* the two super-powers, it could exert considerable psychological influence on European public opinion, and help the Europeans adjust themselves to the painful process of unification. The romantic appeal of 'Independence' and 'Europeanness' combined is not a force to be underestimated.

Conclusion

# THE LIMITS OF EUROPEAN CHOICE

## I

The examination of these six models of a future Western Europe has sought to elicit the stresses and strains, the opportunities and the risks which progression down a particular road would involve. The models have been analysed in terms of their impact on American, Soviet, and East European interests and policies, as well as their implications for Western Europe itself. What general conclusions can be drawn by comparing these findings?

First, the comparative effects on the Atlantic relationship. With which kind of Europe would the United States live most successfully in the 1970s? A revival of the *Partner hip* concept of the original 'Grand Design' is not impossible, but the United States would be unlikely to show the amount of patience and consideration for a uniting Western Europe that a stable relationship of 'equal' partners would require. Conceivably, if the forces of circumstance were to weaken the United States, externally and internally, she might feel the need for a strong military and political partner in any renewal of the Cold War. Otherwise, although she might continue to proclaim her ideal objective to be an equal partnership with a united Western Europe, it is, in fact, a form of dependent Europe which might suit her interests best; always supposing that she retains her position as a universal power and is prepared to exert the leadership which must accompany such a role.

But the relationship with an *Atlanticized Europe*, built on European weakness and resentment, could, in the long term, be dangerously unstable. So too would the American connection with an *Evolutionary Europe*, which, although offering some economic attractions, might prompt the United States to reinsure through bilateral defence arrangements in Western Europe and a policy of preserving the *status quo*.

None of the three other models – *Europe des Etats*, *Fragmented Europe* and *Independent Federal Europe* – would have even a superficial attraction for the United States. Each, in its different way, would increase the sense of American disenchantment with her European allies and might cause the United States drastically to redefine her commitments to Europe (*Europe des Etats* and *Fragmented Europe*), or to withdraw altogether and leave Western Europe to its own devices (*Independent Federal Europe*).

Second, the comparative effects on East–West relations. For the East European states, a Western Europe which is both loose in its structure and independent in its orientation would offer them the greatest freedom of choice and manœuvre within the Communist community: and, conversely, the more rigid the West European structure and the more Atlantic its orientation, the greater would be their dependence on Soviet leadership and control. Thus, both *Atlanticized* and *Partnership Europe* would have a detrimental effect on the trends in Eastern Europe towards acquiring a greater degree of independence. The East Europeans would also react adversely to *Independent Federal Europe*, and would draw closer to the Soviet Union for fear of a powerful West European community or state in which Germany would be seen as the dominating element. The same fear of a situation in which Germany is no longer inside an effective NATO nor moving into a new West European framework, would be generated by *Fragmented Europe*, which otherwise might offer some attraction.

The two models which would appeal most to Eastern Europe would be *Evolutionary Europe* and *Europe des Etats*. The former to the extent that a passive Western Europe, in which Germany remains firmly within the NATO framework, would offer East European countries the widest options for developing economic and other links with the West. The latter, to the extent that it challenged the Soviet hegemony in

Eastern Europe and offered prospects of fruitful economic co-operation with the West; though the instability of Germany's position would be a serious cause for concern.

The pattern of comparable reactions by the Soviet Union would be somewhat different. The Soviet attitude towards *Partnership* and *Atlanticized Europe* would be clear: both would be seen to perpetuate and strengthen the American position in Europe. This she would oppose, unless there had been a marked change in the global balance of power, she was in open conflict with China and was facing a total loss of control over Eastern Europe. Her attitude towards *Independent Federal Europe* would be as suspicious as that of the United States.

On the other hand, the Soviet view of the more loosely structured forms of West European co-operation would be ambivalent; satisfaction with what would be regarded as a set-back to the American position in Europe would be balanced by fear of their attraction to East European countries. This fear would prevail in respect of both *Evolutionary Europe* and *Europe des Etats*; but the former would be the more acceptable as offering the best combination of weakness in the West and the preservation of the *status quo*, without the risk of encouraging a new German nationalism, such as is inherent in *Europe des Etats*.

*Fragmented Europe* would appear to be tailor-made to suit the interests of the Soviet Union, enabling her to gain influence in a weak Western Europe without losing control in the East. But the very instability and unpredictability of such a Europe would be cause for concern, and calculated to impel the Soviet Union to collaborate with the United States in reaching some *modus vivendi* over Europe, for fear of being drawn into inter-European conflicts over which neither super-power could exercise effective control. *Independent Federal Europe* and, to a lesser extent, *Europe des Etats* and *Evolutionary Europe* could all, in varying degrees, lead to similar collaboration between the super-powers.

None of the models, however, would induce the Soviet Union to make substantive concessions in Central Europe and thus bring about a durable settlement of the German problem. With the American position strengthened in *Partnership* and *Atlanticized Europe*, the Soviet reaction would be to tighten the grip on Eastern Germany. *Independent Federal Europe* would have the same effect; the Soviet Union would have no inducement to offer concessions to this new West European state, and it would not be quite powerful enough to exact them. The same would be true, but for opposite reasons, in respect of the weaker European models portrayed in *Evolutionary* or *Fragmented Europe* or again in *Europe des Etats*. Western Europe would not only be incapable of putting any pressure on the Soviet Union to reach a settlement in Europe, but the latter would see no advantage in reaching one if Western Europe already seemed to be drifting in a direction generally favourable to her objectives.

But it would be a mistake to believe that the Soviet leaders would be nicely weighing the advantages and disadvantages of this or that pattern of forces in Western Europe. Their attitude would continue to be governed by the notion that their country was in a state of permanent competition with Western capitalism – the continuance as *Pravda* has recently expressed it of 'an era of irreconcileable ideological struggle between the two opposing systems',[1] and their paramount objective would continue to be to prevent the establishment of a strong centre of power in Western Europe under German 'domination'.

And what of the choices for Western Europe itself? The earlier chapters have been confined primarily to an analysis of the internal consistency, the feasibility of each model and its likely effects. The relative probability of the models and their comparative desirability have been left for examination here.

Europe's own ideal would best be met if the pattern of the relationship between the countries of Western Europe, and the general objectives to which each subscribed, were such as to promote European cohesion, security, and prosperity, without alienating either the United States or the Soviet Union, or jeopardizing conditions of *détente* which could lead to a perma-

[1] L. Onikou, 'Socialism and Democracy', *Pravda*, 19 May 1968.

nent settlement in Central Europe; in other words, to have its cake and eat it.

It is perhaps not surprising to find that none of the models offers a satisfactory solution for Europe as a whole. *Evolutionary Europe* might be tolerable for a time, but it lacks the degree of political solidarity and purpose needed to ensure its own stability or to hold out the prospect of an eventual European settlement. *Atlanticized Europe* might guarantee West Europe's material well-being and security, but it would solidify the divisions of Europe, weaken the individual states in the West, and build up an inheritance of national resentment which could become dangerously explosive. *Europe des Etats*, by alienating the United States, since it would face her with increasing risks if she were associated with its security, would jeopardize Europe's own long-term security, while offering only a fragile promise of an improvement in East–West relations.

*Fragmented Europe*, although presenting the widest range of options in the short-term, would soon lead to a highly unstable situation, with West Germany in a dangerously uncertain position, and the United States and the Soviet Union driven to seek closer collaboration at Europe's expense. A *Partnership Europe*, if it ever mustered the political will to develop a federal structure, could provide Western Europe with the optimum conditions for playing a world-wide role, while ensuring her defences and expanding her industrial power. But, even if a viable formula could be found to preserve the right mixture of equality and inequality within the partnership, the renunciation of German reunification that a Europe moving towards a complete federal structure would require and the probable hardening of Europe's division at least for some time would be a heavy price to pay. The price would be greater still in *Independent Federal Europe*, with the eventual abandonment of West Berlin to East German or Soviet control, and this without any certainty that either the United States or the Soviet Union, or both together, would not use their superior power to curb West Europe's ambitions.

## II

Modelling of this kind cannot, of course, accommodate the half-positions, qualifications, and blurred perspectives which are the reality of international politics. But it does help to expose the broad alternatives, and to confront the policy-makers of today – the politicians, bureaucrats, and industrialists – with the choices they will have to make, especially over the structure of Western Europe's internal association, in order to bring about the kind of Europe they want or to avoid the kind of Europe they do not want.

In determining such choices any changes in the framework of the European balance of power in the 1970s will be of crucial importance. If, for instance, one could assert with confidence that Soviet forces would have left Europe, that the Warsaw Pact would have been disbanded, or that the West European powers would see no necessity for a defence relationship with the United States, then their freedom of choice would expand considerably. But there is no justification for any such forecast, for reasons which we suggested in the Introduction.

Europe is a dangerous place. The smallest of the world's continents, it now contains some 29 states (including both Germanies) each with varying powers of decision-making who deploy between them about 2 million men under arms in Europe, over 25,000 tanks and nearly 12,000 military aircraft, as well as having a large megatonnage of nuclear warheads on their soil. The European balance of power is not autonomous but is an asymmetrical one between a very strong regional power, the Soviet Union, and a universal power, the United States. The European states are part of this balance but they neither created it nor are its central buttresses. What maintains stability in Europe is the central Soviet–American balance, and the European members of it are subject to the very conservative forces which an equation as vast as the central balance, resting as it does on a capacity for mutual destruction on a titanic scale, inevitably perpetuates; what Raymond Aron meant when he said many years ago that the nuclearization of the European balance had led to the 'deceleration of history'.

There may well be minor or superficial changes in the nature both of the central balance and of the European aspect of it during the 1970s. M. Debré, the French Foreign Minister, may well be right in comparing the Czech crisis to a road accident that need not lead to the permanent closure of the road. The events of 1968 need not impede the steady increase in contacts between Eastern and Western Europe. Certain countries, which are not strategically exposed, may decide to opt out of the business of maintaining the European power balance, though the number of countries who can make the choice is limited. The Soviet Union and the United States may well find common ground on restraint in the technology of strategic weapons so that the early 1970s are not blackened by a mutual sense of fear and uncertainty as were the late 1950s. During this period there may well be force reductions, tacitly or explicitly negotiated. But it seems improbable that the next decade will witness the dismantling of the European aspect of the central balance, or that any of the European powers will wish to take action that might risk its collapse.

If there seems likely to be no basic change in the European power structure at least in the early 1970s, what are the choices for Western Europe in the light of the lessons learnt from studying our six models?

(1) We in Western Europe cannot have a strategic nuclear force, operating independently of the United States, without risking a serious increase in tension with the East or causing the United States to prefer to deal with the Soviet Union at our expense. (2) If we wish to promote our own security and independent economic power, we cannot afford to risk the effects of a policy aimed at isolationism and European nationalism. We shall have to pay the price in terms of an increase in European institutionalized co-operation and acceptance of a greater pooling of national contributions in the science-based

and defence-related industries. (3) We cannot have a continued *détente* with the Soviet Union and healthy relations with Eastern Europe without making an effort to achieve an optimum, but limited, amount of cohesion and co-operation in Western Europe (building *inter alia* on the Community structure) and of defence arrangements which include the United States. If a European security system is ever likely to emerge, it will be through the instruments of the two opposing alliances in Europe and not through their disappearance. (4) If some form of federation of Western Europe is a long-term objective, we must also accept the risk of a hardening of the division of Europe and the abandonment of German reunification. (5) If we wish to retain American interest in Europe's problems and American support for specific European interests, we shall have to be prepared to offer something in return: even if it is no more than evidence that West European governments can together research and discuss problems in common to the point where they can offer the United States a coherent European reaction to her own initiatives and developments elsewhere in the world.

Two other broad observations can also be made, which would seem to have a general application, whichever European model is examined. *First*, co-operation which leaves Eastern Europe out in the cold will not be acceptable for West Europeans. It will no longer be possible to think about future relations between the two halves of Europe purely from the standpoint of West European or Atlantic considerations. This will have to be taken into account in any plans to promote integration in Western Europe, even if it is a limiting factor. The Czechoslovak crises of 1968 far from eliminating this consideration underlines its importance. *Second*, the post-war concept of a constitutional federal state as an ultimate goal may appear to Europe's new generation increasingly out of tune with the times, an artificial construction inspired by the European enthusiasts of the 1940s and 1950s. The expression of 'Europeanness' in the 1970s is likely to find other forms than the structured models of the European federalists. A common feature of this new generation is freedom from ideological and nationalist attitudes: 'efficiency, the removal of national barriers, and the prevention of war in Europe are the leading ideas of the rising Europeans'.[2]

It is striking how similar are the forecasts about the mixed motives, flexible relationships and overlapping structures which will characterize the Europe of the 1970s. 'The Europe of tomorrow . . . is likely to be rather blurred at the edges, with various kinds of special arrangements, south to the Mediterranean and Africa, east to the neutrals and perhaps some of the smaller countries of Eastern Europe.'[3] 'In the early 1970s Europe will probably be neither the divided Europe of the Cold War nor the restored, reunified or integrated Europe of a continental balance of power, of collective security, of a general settlement, or of a political federation. Rather it will be the "mixed motive" Europe of "imperfect partnership" and "incomplete antagonism", of overlapping groupings and cross-cutting alignments.'[4] 'To deal with its European interlocuteurs in the 1970s America will require a diplomacy more engaged in identifying and reconciling diverging interests, and less with the reconstruction of Europe in terms of some ideal image.'[5] 'A full-fledged West European federation is neither conceivable in the near future nor likely to have much appeal, since it would probably be absorbed by problems of internal organization and much more difficult to open to the East. Something different is needed, more flexible so as to be effective.'[6]

It would almost seem as though, over the past two years, the advocates of this, or that, clearly structured pattern of association

[2] J. L. Richardson, *Germany and the Atlantic Alliance* (Cambridge, Mass. and London: Harvard University Press and Oxford University Press, 1966), p. 212.

[3] M. Camps, *European Unification in the Sixties* (London: Oxford University Press, 1967), p. 235.

[4] P. Hassner, *Change and Security in Europe: Part I*, Adelphi Paper No. 45 (London: ISS, 1968), p. 24

[5] Anthony Hartley, *Interplay*, May 1968.

[6] Stanley Hoffman, *Gulliver's Troubles* (New York and London: Praeger-mill Pallmall, 1968), p. 531.

for Western Europe and for its relations with the United States, have lost heart; baffled by the perplexing way in which new post-war institutions have developed, and confused by the absence of any clear sign-posts to the future. The student of international affairs today faces a difficult task: to make sense and order out of a shifting kaleidoscope of economic and political impulses and restrictions, with old fears and habits mingling with new aspirations and possibilities; and a realization of the inadequacy of these post-war institutions matching an uncertainty as to how to adapt them. In the words of T. C. Schelling, 'the time for the Grand Schemes is over. We are moving out of our architectural period in Europe into the age of manœuvre.'[7]

This 'architectural period' was the response to two special post-war phenomena: the Soviet and Communist threat to West Europe's security and the Marshall Plan's offer of aid to an impoverished Europe. To meet both these challenges highly organized forms of co-operation were seen to be necessary. NATO was created to provide the machinery of integration for the American alliance with Western Europe against the Soviet threat. The OEEC was created to enable the Europeans collectively to plan the distribution of American aid. In both cases the chosen instruments were intergovernmental, but of a more intimate nature than anything previously achieved in peace time – permanently organized intergovernmental co-operation in the pursuit of well-defined common interests.

The third feature of this architectural period, and the most ambitious, has been the introduction of 'supranational' institutions, initiated with the ECSC and extended to Euratom and the EEC, and characterized by what has come to be known as the 'community system': a novel experiment, peculiar to Western Europe, differing in kind from either the intergovernmental systems of functional co-operation (e.g. GATT and the IMF) or the ideal of a constitutional federal state of Europe in which certain powers are granted to the central government and others reserved by the individual states.

[7] Quoted in Hoffmann, *op. cit.*, p. 495.

But it is becoming increasingly questionable whether this 'community system', as it has developed, is the most appropriate form in which Western Europe's full potential could be shaped to meet the problems of the 1970s. In the first place, and regardless of the personal antipathy of President de Gaulle, it is doubtful whether the Community organization in Brussels should be extended to embrace the political fields of foreign policy and defence. The political will is clearly lacking today and none of the foreseeable trends suggests that the European leaders of the 1970s will be able to invoke sufficient enthusiasm to make this a possibility tomorrow.

On the contrary, the Eurocrats are probably doing a disservice to the 'community idea', by insisting that it must inexorably lead to a politically federated Europe. It is no doubt true that the initiators of the ECSC meant it 'to form part of a European Political Community together with other communities in other sectors of economic life and in the field of defence; the explicit intention being to transform this cluster of communities eventually into a European Federation'.[8] But the constant harping on the community method as the all-embracing panacea, and on the federal goal as Europe's eventual destiny has already begun to be counter-productive. It will only serve to increase the caution of the leaders of the major European powers, who will be reluctant to pledge their governments to open-ended commitments from which they could not withdraw; and it will provide European civil servants with the pretext for claiming that such widely extended forms of supranationalism cannot reasonably be adopted in the near future and should, therefore, be left to the harmless imaginings of the political theorists.

Indeed, it is a pity that the Eurocrats have come to think and speak of the future Western Europe in terms of a new power bloc, a federalized super-state constructed out of its territorial and national parts, and welded together through the independent authority of the Community institutions in Brussels.

[8] Dr J.W. Beijen, 'United Europe: Federal or Supranational', *Internationale Spectator*, The Hague, April 1965, p. 461.

For this is still the limited, national state writ large; and there
is little in the analysis in the preceding chapters to suggest that
this will provide the optimum prescription for solving Europe's
problems in the next decade. Federalism is 'a form of national,
not of international, government; and its direct relevance to
the problems of Europe is by no means clear'.[9] Existing
federations are all national federations which came into being
under conditions very different from the intimate and complex
intergovernmental activities through which the separate
nation states of Europe would have to be united in the future.
Moreover, none of the present six governments of the EEC
countries, nor such potential members as Britain, have clearly
stated how they see the end product of closer political and
economic integration.[10] For if there is to be a political union
including defence and foreign policy, there must also be a
central executive authority for decision-making; and it is hard
to see this evolving naturally from the steady application of the
'community system' to the economic and technological problems of Western Europe in the 1970s. Even the more modest
hopes that a common market would lead to the integration of
the European economy through the merger of European
corporations across national boundaries, have proved un-
founded. On the contrary, the corporate merger movement
in Western Europe is taking place either within national
boundaries or else between European and American firms. It
is American, not European, companies which are rationalizing
and integrating the European economy. And the giant international companies themselves may even be slipping out of the
control of national governments.

Secondly, the economic trends, on which hopes for political
union were set, point not to a tidy framework for Europe's

[9] Max Beloff, *Europe and the Europeans* (London: Chatto and Windus,
1957), p. 276.
[10] 'Only on the basis of a real political and economic unity in Europe can
our continent heal its divisions and regain, through that ever-widening unity,
its rightful influence for peace', Mr Harold Wilson, House of Commons,
27 August 1968. (H. of C. Deb., Vol. 769, Col. 1283.)

political and economic unity in the 1970s, but towards a motley arrangement of overlapping interests and cross-cutting alignments: 'a relationship among the highly-industrialized countries which is marked by great freedom of movement for goods, capital and people; fairly strict codes of conduct restraining enterprises and states from distorting competition or acquiring unfair advantages; and close co-ordination of fiscal and monetary policies'; not an exclusive European or Atlantic system, but a 'network of economic arrangements', with Canada, Japan, and Australia as full participants and other industrialized countries in Eastern Europe and Latin America progressively drawn into it. [11]

We are now entering the 'age of manœuvre' where diversity and interdependence are beginning to replace the old system of imperial dominance and spheres of influence, and where Europe's needs can probably no longer be satisfied exclusively by any one of the structures examined in this book. Despite the reassertion of the nation state there is a growing realization that the interests of Western states now overflow in all directions, and that the governments of the highly developed countries will have to find a new relationship with each other. Irrespective of political relations, new patterns of co-ordination will probably emerge, simply in order to avoid an economic break-down and to meet the demands of the 'crisis of modernization' which seems to be an environment common to all European societies.

The national framework is clearly 'too big now for some purposes that need smaller units; too small for other functions that need a supranational scale'.[12] But some coherent structure is required that will still enable Europe to keep in sight the goal of economic and political unity, while remaining sufficiently open-ended to match and adapt itself to the possible shifts in the balance of power, and the cross-currents of the

[11] M. Camps, 'Is "Europe" Obsolete?', *International Affairs*, July 1968, pp. 441–2.
[12] U. Kitzinger, 'Britain's Crisis of Identity', *Journal of Common Market Studies*, June 1968, p. 353.

economic and financial forces that have been discussed here. The use of a variety of approaches will be the key to success.

## III

Such a Europe might be found in a strengthened form of functional co-operation; modelled on the community method, but neither seeking to embrace the totality of political responsibilities in the field of foreign policy and defence, nor looking to a federal super-state as its ultimate objective. In addition to the three existing European Communities, which might either include Britain and the Scandinavian countries or provide the inner core of a wider association with the EFTA and other countries, there might be a limited Defence Community and a Technological Community, both with supranational characteristics but depending on the degree of common interest that could be mobilized. There could be a central European monetary system but again clearly limited to a specific purpose and closely co-ordinated with the fiscal and monetary policies of the United States, and other industrialized countries. Common institutions can only be developed concurrently with common interests; they cannot create them. In some cases, for instance communication or transportation or common energy programmes, the community method might be adapted to permit the association of countries in Eastern Europe or outside the continent of Europe. In other cases, the particular function could be adequately performed through intergovernmental co-operation, or it might be thought to touch too closely on the core of national sovereignty to be treated in any other way

Since the final objective would not be the closed and rigid pattern of a federal constitution, the system would remain open. The participating states would retain their identities and would be free to develop their bilateral relations with Eastern Europe, complementary to the limited functional bodies of which they were also members. Canada, for example, could fit into this system, as well as those East European states which might acquire more freedom to co-operate economically with the West while remaining strategically and politically within the Soviet system.

The defence aspect, however, might be more difficult to handle. The North Atlantic Treaty could remain unchanged and also the formal structure of NATO itself. This Europe would not be of a kind to handle its own nuclear armoury, nor would she need to do so. The United States, being industrially and monetarily interlocked with Western Europe at the functional level could not contemplate its abandonment, and would retain a strategic force for its protection. The British and French nuclear strategic forces might lose their significance or even be allowed to fall into disuse, in the absence of any European political structure for controlling them. On the other hand, the functional co-operation between the West Europeans on specific aspects of conventional defence, being of a supranational character, would help to adjust the balance within an avowedly unequal partnership. Such a European entity might contribute to the functional diversification of power and to a return to a moderate system where the use and possession of nuclear force would not be the constant theme of international politics.[13]

The watchword and the motive of this mixed European system, partly inter-governmental, partly supranational, would be 'efficiency': how to extract the maximum benefits at the minimum cost in a world of increasing diversity and technical complexity. In such a plurality of international organization the Atlantic Alliance and the European Communities would each make their indispensible contribution to Europe's security and prosperity. But they would lose their special devotees, the 'Atlanticists' and the 'European federalists'. Unlike a federal system which is, by definition, closed and exclusive, such a functional system would be flexible and open. It could absorb changes in membership and extend itself into new fields, without a publicized confrontation with high

[13] Hoffmann, *op. cit.*, p. 536.

national policies and without offending the pride of national sovereignty.[14] Governments would be enticed by the carrot of cost-benefits and technical efficiency into participating in new supranational experiments, where the task is clearly limited and any loss of sovereignty circumscribed. It would be a modest form of federalism *à la carte*, where each move forward would be seen to satisfy a specific need.

Profiting from the discussion in the preceding chapters one could construct an 'ideal' Europe which would be an amalgam of all the positive features of the six West European models while omitting all their awkward elements. This could be a sort of egg-laying pig which produces wool and milk. But it would not be a very realistic animal.

The present sketch of a possible European structure in the 1970s is not intended to be yet another model; it is rather an attempt at a forecast of the likely forces at work and of the way in which common tasks will probably be dealt with. It is, in a sense, a resurrection of some of the ideas of the early exponents of functionalism; in particular David Mitrany who was expounding the thesis, with remarkable prescience, twenty-five years ago,[15] though as a global, not just a European, prescription. As with all imaginative new approaches to political problems some of the supporters of the functionalist theory have exaggerated its merits. There are clearly limits beyond which the functionalist organization of international society cannot go. Although the nation state may have become perforated at many points, it will be a long time before the sphere of national politics and the state's role within it can be restricted as narrowly as some theorists have advocated.[16]

[14] David Mitrany, 'The Prospect of Integration: Federal or Functional', *Journal of Common Market Studies*, Dec. 1965.

[15] He defines functionalism as a union with joint, but limited, liability for a particular activity. The number of such unions is not predetermined; none is contractually conditioned on others; the structure and jurisdiction may vary from one to another; and so may the associated partners (e.g., ECSC; Antarctica; N.P.T.).

[16] See E. Haas, *Beyond the Nation State* (Stanford, Calif.; Stanford University Press, 1964).

But the functional solution bears the smack of reality as a general prescription for the world in the 1970s, and not just for the sophisticated West Europeans. 'The existing European Communities with their links to associated Africa, the Commonwealth consultative machinery, and other existing regional bodies could form, with revamped organs of the United Nations, a network of overlapping circles, untidy perhaps, but with an untidiness that reflects the functional character of each body, tailored in composition and structure precisely to fulfil a particular concrete task.'[17]

It can, of course, be criticized on several scores. It does not, for example, offer any solution to the German problem. But then no structural change in Western Europe can, by itself, produce that. At least it does not militate against it, as do some of the West European models we have examined; and it might be positively helpful by reason of the flexibility of its institutions and their adaptability to any shifts there may be in the relations between East European countries and the Soviet Union.

Another criticism might be that it looks unrealistic in the light of Soviet behaviour towards Czechoslovakia in August 1968. But the basic security guarantees of Western Europe would not have been undermined, while all options would be kept open for the future, if the process of *détente* were resumed. It is a system that can make allowance for diplomatic and political set-backs without risking a reversion to *Fragmented Europe*, or a dangerous disillusionment which could shatter some of the other models.

Or it might be criticized on the score that it would deprive the European Community system, as it has been developed through the organizations in Brussels, of the political drive and inspiration needed to impel the governments along the road to political unity. The Community in Brussels, it could be argued, would become just a bureaucratic business manager for the economies of the Continent and the EEC 'a sort of

[17] U. Kitzinger, *The European Common Market and Community* (London: Routledge and Kegan Paul, 1967), p. 216.

secular church whose priests were powerful but in whose religion no one really believed any more'.[18] If this were the effect it would have to be accepted. The Community system of the Brussels model should not be the exclusive prescription for European co-operative ventures.

## IV

The mixed, functional Europe suggested here would be a more modest Europe than many people have hoped and worked for.

*Functional Europe* may sound tame stuff to a younger generation fretting under the conventional wisdom of their elders. But it might, nevertheless, prove to be a more realistic Europe for the 1970s. And in fact it offers considerable intellectual and political challenge. For it may require a profound change in our concept of international co-operation. There are problems of public concern that central governments now rarely handle successfully, higher education appears to be one, urban planning another; there might be much to be said for a professional confederation of European higher education authorities, and already the 'governments' of the great megalopolizes have made clear that they understand each other's problems more readily, and can contribute more effectively to their solution, than central governments can do. Two companies can agree to build an aircraft very easily, but the whole problem becomes bureaucratized and delayed if it is handled through central governments. On the other hand, there are some traditional functions of the state where, in Europe at least, it may no longer be efficient merely to aggregate the resources of governments, and a higher form of authority may be required. The point has been accepted in relation to energy; it looks as if it is becoming true of defence, one of the central historic functions of the nation state in its old conception.

[18] David Calleo, *Europe's Future: The Grand Alternatives* (New York; Horizon Press, 1965), p. 66.

Finally, the objectives of such an experimental Europe are closely related to a question that has rapidly risen to the surface in recent years and will stay there, and not only in Europe. Can the highly industrialized states sustain or recover a quality in their national life which not only satisfies the new generation, but can act as an example or attractive force to other societies? If Western Europe can develop successful techniques of urban government, can expand education without generating disorder, can use its land resources with skill, can by techniques of devolution minimize racial and ethnic conflict, but still plan on a big scale those projects which require massive capital or a mass market, then it will have achievements to record which will sustain the interest of the United States, and excite that of Eastern Europe, including eventually the Soviet Union. But if the quality of European life decays so will its interest for the world, whatever the structure of its political relations.